Sykes-Pico

Sykes-Picot – 1916

Acting for the Dotted Lines.

BASSIL A. Mardelli

Sykes-Picot - 1916

Acting for the Dotted Lines

Copyright © 2017 Bassil A. Mardelli

First Print: June 15, 2017.

Second Print: April 5, 2018.

Third Print: November 15, 2020.

ISBN- 13-978-1548039769

ISBN- 10-1548039764 (Proof 72256950R00105)

CreateSpace books may be ordered through booksellers or by contacting:

CreateSpace, a DBA of On-Demand Publishing, LLC.
An Amazon Company
CreateSpace.
4900 La Cross Road.
North Charleston, SC 29406

Printed in the United States of America

CreateSpace.

Sykes-Picot has been thought of before, but the challenge is to think of it again

TABLE OF CONTENTS

Prologue

In the First World War, The Arabs fought the Turks alongside the Allies – England, France, Russia, and later, the United States - but were clueless about the Allies' postwar designs.

In a series of secret talks that began in 1915 and concluded in May 1916, known as Sykes-Picot,[1] Britain and France carved up the Arab territories that were part of the Ottoman Empire. The Russian Czar had already assented without having any active participation in it.

With or without Sykes-Picot, the entire Levant and Arabia had already been divided.
Sykes-Picot was, principally, dotted lines with colored zones on maps fitting military geography.
England and France used to push the Germans out of the Middle East and the Mediterranean region.
Allied armies, manned by Muslims, were ready to fight the German *infidels*.
It was the same in Germany, whose Ottoman allies played on the Sunni majority's confessional sentiments to fight the French and British *infidels*.
Hence, it was a war between Muslims allied to the three competing powers who, their propagandists, successfully applied the call for *JIHAD* to the maximum.

Centuries of conflicts between rival chieftains, tribes, families, and clans, but also between Turks, Kurds, and Arabs, left Mark Sykes and Georges Picot no choice but 'dotting-lines.'

---

[1] Sykes-Picot, had taken the name of the two of its 'lieutenants' – Sir Mark Sykes, an English gentleman who had died in Paris, and Georges Picot. In 1919, Picot had been the High Commissioner of France in Syria.

They drew those lines and colored zones for two primary purposes.
The first is to protect the rear of their advancing armies as they progressed in WWI's difficulties.
The second: to streamline the activities of their troops.

Sykes and Picot wanted to avoid the ordeal of Muslim forces, fighting for and employed by France and England, on the spur of the moment, exchanging 'friendly fires' when advancing through the vast lands falling within their military operations.

I have referred to many declassified archives of the British Foreign Ministry by expanding for this new edition.
I examined many documents in the context of other statements made by French, British, German, and American political leaders in the formal analysis of the European international situation between the Entente Cordial – 1904 and First World War – 1914-1918.

Bassil A. Mardelli
Beirut, March 30, 2018

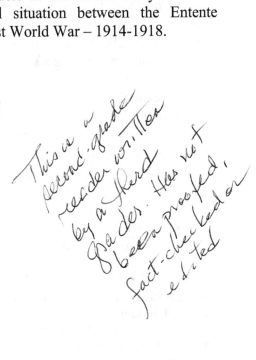

Chapter 1. *Mark Sykes.*

In 1903, although very young at 24, Captain Mark Sykes had already made his mark not only as a soldier but as a litterateur and traveler. When at Cambridge, he published a paper called *The Snarl.*

He contributed to various newspapers and wrote a burlesque on the English military service issued with the King's permission and made a great vogue in the service.[2]

In 1903 Captain Mark Sykes married Edith Violet, third daughter of Sir John Gorst, at York. The marriage had been of some interest to Americans.

It was believed that Mark Sykes - *a precarious youth of twelve or fourteen* - happened to supply, unconsciously, much of the material as the original of Kipling's youth who fell overboard and made a hero in that excellent novel, "Captain Courageous."[3]

> Captain Sykes is the son of Sir Tatton Sykes, an immensely wealthy Yorkshire baronet, who has gone abroad for the past fifty years or more, wearing two or three suits of clothes and three or four overcoats to keep him warm.

> Sir Tatton is well known in New York and in the West, where he owns mines. Lady Sykes, Mark's mother, is, of course, remembered in New York

---

[2] The New York Times, Sunday, November 22, 1903.

[3] Rudyard Kipling was born on December 30, 1865, in Bombay, India. He was educated in England but returned to India in 1882. A decade later, Kipling settled in Brattleboro, Vermont, where he wrote The Jungle Book (1894), among a host of other works that made him hugely successful.

drawing-rooms. She is one of the Cavendish Bentincks,[4] who have had so much intercourse with American society for generations.

They used to travel to and fro on the Atlantic in former years. And it was remembered about ten or twelve years ago, the young man who is now married was on board the Teutonic[5] – a precarious youth of twelve or fourteen, fitting in and out of the smoking-room, making things hot for the passengers.

There was a big storm, and Master Mark, with a new suit of clothes on him, was caught up by a gigantic wave and washed up and down along the lee scuppers. When he emerged, he looked like a soaked chimneysweep. The scene made a great impression upon Kipling, who was on board. Hence the writing of his novel *"Captain Courageous."*

From 1905 to 1907, now Sir Mark Sykes was an honorary attaché at the British Embassy in Constantinople. But official life little attached him. His custom was to make long and lonely journeys through Turkey in Asia, running many risks, violating all diplomatic precedents, and always returning loaded with valuable information gathered first-hand from little-known places. In this manner and with these objects in view, he visited five Turkish provinces, collecting the material for several

---

[4] The Bentinck family is a prominent family belonging to both Dutch and British nobility. Its members have served in the armed forces and as ambassadors and politicians, including Governor General of India and Prime Minister of the United Kingdom.

[5] The RMS Teutonic was a steamship built for the White Star Line in Belfast and was the first armed merchant cruiser, launched in January 1889 (not to be confused with the Titanic).

books: "Through Five Turkish Provinces," "Dar-ul-Islam," "The Caliphs Last Heritage," to name but a few.[6]

French, Turkish, and Arabic he spoke fluently, though it is improbable that he ever received formal tutoring in them. As his method of travel, his procedure in the study was straightforward and direct. In the choice of routes for travel, he said that he pursued the invariable principle of "following his nose over those portions of the map which were the whitest or most rich in notes of interrogation and dotted lines."

In 1906, Sir Mark Sykes received the Foreign Office's thanks and the Army Council for work done with the Turkish Expeditionary Force.
He mapped the northwest region of Mesopotamia[7] and the desert south of Jerusalem.
In his travels, Mark Sykes rode 14,000 miles (22,530 Kilometers) and produced maps of 5,000 miles (8,047 Kilometers) of previously unknown roads in Asiatic Turkey. He was a leading authority on the Baghdad Railway question.[8]

Sir Mark Sykes was hailed as a Unionist Member for Central Hull at a by-election in 1911.
Before the election, he had twice fought the Buckrose Division of Yorkshire. In the recent General Election, he earned a majority of 10,371 over Rev. R. M. Redward.

---

[6] The latter was reviewed in *The Times Literary Supplement* of November 15, 1915.

[7] Mesopotamia: ancient name for the land that lies between the Tigris and Euphrates rivers (in modern Iraq), from Greek Mesopotamia (kora), literally "a country between two rivers," - meso "middle" plus potamos "river."

[8] The Berlin-Baghdad Railway as a cause for World War One, by Arthur P. Maloney Prepared at New York University, 1959.

It is worthwhile noting that he was abroad at the time of the election and his election address had to be telegraphed from Cairo.

His first speech in the House of Commons contributed to a debate on foreign affairs and earned him the rare distinction of the Prime Minister's congratulations.

Before entering the House of Commons, Mark Sykes had served with the 5th Yorkshire Regiment in the South African War. He was mentioned in the dispatches and received two medals.

In Ireland, he served with Mr. Wyndham and was an active advocate of 'conciliation,' a graceful skill that he used later with Georges Picot.

He developed a somewhat independent attitude on the old party-political issues. He had been known to say that he would never have accepted office in any Government even had the opportunity come.

Sir Mark Sykes was a man of remarkable versatility and shone equally as a raconteur and caricaturist.

Besides being a great traveler, a soldier, and an author, he was a first-rate amateur actor and a mimic of uncanny accuracy. Wherever he went, he carried with him an atmosphere of the East. His country seat at Sledmere was filled with Oriental curiosities. When he rebuilt Sledmere after a fire demolished the place in 1911, he had constructed to his design a Turkish bath, for which tiles were specially brought from Konia.

Sir Mark took little interest in horse racing before the death of his father.[9] However, he fully realized the great

---

[9] Sir Tatton Sykes, Fifth Baronet, was born in 1826, and died on May 4, 1913, at the age of 87. Tatton was extremely wealthy landowner, racehorse breeder and church builder and eccentric. At the age of 48 he married Jessica Cavendish-Bentinck, Mark's mother who was thirty years younger than his father and it is believed the marriage was not a happy one. It is through this marriage that the Sykes are related

traditions of the Sledmere Stud and, deciding that its continuity should not be broken, placed it under the control of his cousin, Henry Cholmondeley. The latter had assisted Sir Tatton in its management for something like 20 years. The annual sale of the Sledmere yearlings at Doncaster used to be one of the racing season features, attracting buyers from all parts of the world.

At Sledmere, he was a good and popular landlord and had recently completed an elaborate scheme for the cottage's remodeling on his estate and the provision of new ones. It was to have been put into operation at the end of the war.

In a piece written by La Marquise De Fontenoy on February 18, 1911, The Times-Dispatch, Virginia, reports about Mark Sykes who had just been granted colonelcy and promoted to the lieutenant of the battalions of the Yorkshire Regiment:

> He [...] has inherited none of his eccentric parent's oddities, Sir Tatton, who won the Derby with Spearmint in 1906, is almost as well-known as his wife in this country, which they have repeatedly visited.

Mark Sykes is the *only* son and *heir* of Sir Tatton and Lady Sykes.

> They *[Marks' parents]* are judicially separated but remain on entirely friendly terms. The judicial separation was preceded by an immense amount of litigation, mostly of a financial character. After fighting each other all day in the courts, on every variety of subject, each insisted that the other was more or less mentally irresponsible. Still, they would return home together, presiding at the same dinner table, entertaining large parties of friends,

---

indirectly to Queen Elizabeth II, through a great-grandfather.

breakfast together the next morning, and then proceed to the law courts, in different conveyances it is true, to resume the legal proceedings against one another.

It was one of the many oddities of his parents that he accepted over the years.

Lady Sykes's appearances in court - and they have been numerous, have never affected her popularity. Her social prestige, or her unfailing good humor, especially in the witness box, where she invariably referred to her 'timeworn' husband as "that old dear, whose "peculiarities" she alone was able to understand. [10]

Oddly, nobody had thought of mentioning to Lady Sykes about the recent controversy of what was known as "social journalism." For Mark's mother was, for some time, the owner, publisher, and editress of a London Society Journal, which for its boldness of speech, the discussion of life in Mayfair, and for its general raciness, was without parallel. Naturally, it was brought to an untimely end by a rain of libel suits.

For Mark, wealth would have been an excellent thing as long as it meant power, leisure, and liberty. But he was never left alone. Hence, he would not leave his rivals alone, and this attitude caused him to find entertainment nor freedom nowhere. However, he found power and basked in it as long as it meant adventures and intelligence collection to his government.

In a nutshell, Sir Mark Sykes was like Lawrence of Arabia except that the latter was a commoner.

---

[10] Saturday, February 18, 1911. The Times-Dispatch, Virginia. (by La Marquise De Fontenoy)

The newly-promoted Lieutenant-Colonel Mark Sykes served for a time as attaché of the English embassy at Constantinople.

There, he did a considerable amount of exploring, having performed several standard works of travel to his credit, and could furnish many valuable reports to the Intelligence Department of the British army.

Upon the outbreak of the First World War – July 28, 1914 - Sir Mark raised a battalion of the Yorkshire Regiment. He was expecting to accompany it from France when he received personal orders from Lord Kitchener that his services were urgently required elsewhere.

As a special emissary, he made two crucial journeys.

The first was to Petrograd, the Caucasus, and the Headquarters of the Grand Duke.

The second journey was to Aden, Basra, and Kut-el-Amara.[11] Satisfied with having raised a battalion of fighting men, he turned his attention to transport and sent France a train of horse-drawn wagons.

---

[11] The Siege of Kut Al Amara (7 December 1915 – 29 April 1916), also known as the First Battle of Kut, was the besieging of an 8,000 strong British-Indian garrison in the town of Kut, 160 kilometers (100 mi) south of Baghdad, by the Ottoman Army. In 1915 its population was around 6,500.

Chapter 2. *"What of the Future of Jerusalem?"*

Deep in his heart, Mark Sykes found that any strategies concerning Constantinople and Jerusalem would be challenging to implement without the tacit agreement of the Turks.

Four years before the world war, travelers *marched* from Adana's city in southern Turkey to Aleppo, in northern Syria, about 116 Miles without an escort; nowhere did the traveler meet with more kindness or less danger of molestation than in Asiatic Turkey. Of course, however, lurking thieves occasionally were encountered in these lonely regions. But the strategy of establishing the Tripoli-Baghdad railroad stayed the darling of the British, for they wanted to defeat the Berlin-Baghdad Railway built by the Germans in 1903 and through which means they tried to construct a port in the Persian Gulf. To the British, and Mark Sykes, the beautiful port of Tripoli lying in the sight of the eternal snows and near the cedars of Lebanon was inferior as a harbor to Alexandretta, but it was sufficient for its purpose.

Alexandretta is almost a middle-road between Adana and Aleppo. Britain schemed to expand the Berlin-Baghdad Railway line from Aleppo by Homs to Beirut, and another from Beirut to Damascus.

There would be a connection with Haifa's port (near Acre) via Lake Tiberias from Damascus. There would also be a short line from Jerusalem to Jaffa. Soon after, there would be a line from Jerusalem through Samaria (Palestine) to join the Damascus-Haifa line. And the Homs-Tripoli line would continue along the Euphrates valley Baghdad, which would indeed be cheaper and probably more useful than the better known Berlin-Baghdad Railway to the north.

A valuable extension would be a line from Aleppo to the magnificent Bay of Alexandretta, and Jerusalem might be connected with the Mecca line.

This remarkable enterprise, which was due to the late Sultan Abdul Hamid II initiative, was professedly a "holy railway." It is intended to provide the Muslim pilgrims with a comfortable and rapid conveyance to the sacred places. As mentioned before, since 1906, Mark Sykes had been a leading authority on the Baghdad Railway question.

The idea of planning to connect a railroad from Jerusalem with the Mecca line had been superb, and by all means, would offend the Germans, for it would deprive them of an active card relating to the Holy Lands. And at the same time, Sykes wanted to avoid any action that might irritate the Turks.

Up until 1912, apart from the Hijaz mainline that runs on the eastern boundary, there were two railways in Palestine. The short-range of 54 Miles from Jaffa to Jerusalem owned by a French company. France also held the Damascus-Haifa line, touching south Lake-Galilee and passing through Esdraelon's plain (Jezreel Valley - Palestine).

Simultaneously, there were three new schemes for completing the Germans' lines: the French and the British competed in 1912.

The first – which had begun by German supervision – was for another branch of the Hijaz from Afouleh, a station near Haifa, through Nablus to Jerusalem, which would only provide the tourist with secure communication. It would also serve the most productive districts of Palestine. Such a scheme would offer the Germans an outlet at the Mediterranean Sea.

The second scheme was for a branch of the Hijaz from As-Salt, in the Trans-Jordan country, to Jerusalem, which would again be serviceable for tourists and open up the

Dead Sea region's mineral wealth, which was engaging the attention of several European business enterprises.

The third was: a line along the coast linking Haifa on the north to Beirut through Tyre and Sidon. And on the south to Jaffa and Gaza through the plain of Sharon – a section of the coastal plain in Palestine - was restored to Jewish colonists' ancient fruitfulness.

At that time, it was reported that a German company had obtained a concession for the railway, which would naturally be continued to Al-Arish on the Egyptian frontier, and thence through El-Kantara on the Suez Canal to Port Said.

But what about Constantinople?

On Saturday, March 22, 1913, the Catholic Advance found Mark Sykes, one of the very few Catholic MP's exerting himself in defense of the Turks in a crisis like the present. An inspired press wrote a great deal regarding rumored Bulgarian and Serbian "atrocities" during the Christian armies' recent victorious march. Now Mark Sykes came forward with a remote communication to the "TIMES," in which he refuted any awful acts "perpetrated by the Turks:"

> If the Turks had committed the atrocities, Europe would have been on fire. The Turks have many allies amongst the Jews and Freemasons who control the European press, and the Turk, as we have already seen, does not mind what excuse he uses to gain time when the fortune of war is going against him. To those who know the Christian nations of the Balkans, such as European Catholic officers serving with the Bulgarian army, these tales do not ring true. In short, we do not believe in the so-called atrocities perpetrated on the Turk.

17

There were reasons why the Bulgarian Army wanted to enter Constantinople. Therein is situated the grandest and noblest ancient Christian edifice, ruined and desecrated by the Turks in 1453. To the Christians of Eastern Europe, the magnificent old church of St Sophia is like the Temple of Jerusalem to the Jews. Its desecration and use as a mosque have been an insult, a deep and lasting wound to the Bulgarians.

It dealt a massive blow to Christianity in the East, and the aim of the Christian *races* there has been to avenge that insult, and once more restore the old Church to its ancient and original use.

Consequently, Mark Sykes feared his friendship with the Turks might not survive what comes.

In 1913, the First Balkan War atrocities, October 1912 - May 1913, brought to ruin the Bulgarians in Thrace, Macedonia, and Asia Minor. The Ottoman policy of ethnic *(cultural and racial)* suppression in Southern Macedonia which – Serbia, Romania, Greece, Montenegro - was applied with a high ferocity from the start of the First Balkan War and led to the liberation of the Balkan peoples from Ottoman domination, in which Bulgaria and Greece were allies. It was a racial war for dominance.

During the second war in the Balkans, June - August 1913, Bulgarian ethnic suppression in Southern Macedonia was applied with great ferocity. Indeed, the last Balkan war changed the deck of the belligerent cards – Serbia, Romania, Greece, Montenegro, and the Ottomans – causing many ethnic (cultural and racial) differences resurfaced and lasted until the beginning of the world war.

These peculiar belligerencies were dependent upon prolonged ethnic preparations - convulsions whereby an 'old' race, the Greek, was conquered by a new, the Turks. This time, the Greeks charged that Turkish 'imperialism' forces were attempting to make the

Christians all over the Empire scapegoats in the struggle between liberalism and reaction. The Greeks set that the Turks were using Islam to divert the Muslim people's minds from their real interests to a religious war. The benefits of most Non-Turkish Muslims were "fighting for freedom from the Turkish yokes."

But had conditions in the Balkan anything to do with Jerusalem? A lot, in the mind of Mark Sykes, because both were reeking with unrest. The former suffered from *Racism* against the Turks, and the latter from latent *Fanaticism,* bursting with repressed racial animosity. Jerusalem was paving the way for a new Crusade. If allowed to go on as it was in 1913 and prior, Palestine was destined to be the battlefield of the religions, much worse than the old days in Constantinople and the present Balkan arena.

During 1916-1917, there had been a loud outcry to internationalize Jerusalem. It was announced that a significant German company had been formed to construct an electric power-station near the waterfalls Tel-Shahab in Syria. The power was to be used for working the Damascus-Jerusalem Railway and for lighting and industrial purposes in the district.
But there had also been other schemes for Palestine and Jerusalem for far-reaching socio-political purposes.

Mark Sykes was a refined and useful platform speaker, and probably the best speech of his life was made in December 1917, in Manchester, at a Zionist meeting held just before the fall of Jerusalem.
Meanwhile, the British were trying to establish themselves in Palestine by inspiring a Zionist community to create a stable British buffer state before Egypt. They promised Palestine to the Zionists in 1917, and the world applauded. The world did not realize that the Zionists were a pawn in the British game in Syria. In 1919, even

the British themselves in Palestine were beginning to see the troubles that would inevitably follow any attempt at realizing the Zionist project.

The London Bureau of the Zionist Organization had issued a statement in which it said:

> It was Sir Mark Sykes's political imagination and his unique position of authority on questions relating to the Near East that made him into one of the collaborators in issuing Mr. Balfour's famous declaration of November 2, 1917, in which the British Government promised its aid in the establishment of a Jewish Palestine.

> Since then, he had devoted himself to translating the Declaration into practical politics, and scarcely a month ago, he was in Palestine helping in laying the foundations for the new life of our people. Since his return to Paris, he was engaged in the last task to advocate the Zionist idea in all quarters interested in Palestine's future.

On January 21, 1918, The Wilmington Morning Star wrote: "As soon as peace is made and Holy Land free of Turkish Blight, all races will look to Jerusalem," says Sir Mark Sykes.
The Arabs are remarkably generous in their appreciation of a good speech. They are ready to predict future political distinction for anyone who makes a statement that soars beyond the debate's ordinary level.
The comment Mark Sykes had made about Palestine and Jerusalem resonated well. The subject of Palestine was mentioned hundreds of times before. Still, Mark Sykes' phrases were so finely remarked and displayed a breadth and dignity that they won approval not only from the Arab audience but also from some Jews, albeit to a lesser degree.

20

The Associated Press of December 30, 1918, notes:

> "I believe that Jerusalem after the war will become the moral center of the world," said Sir Mark Sykes, a British authority on the affairs of the Near East, in an interview.

> "There is today throughout the world," he explained, "a deep-rooted desire that this war shall be the last. But if this hope is to be realized, there must be some force that will control nations. People talk of The Hague Conference, and yet we know that hitherto these conferences have been, and maybe again in the future, just hypocritical conversations between lawyers, diplomats, and soldiers preparing for new hostilities."

Once more, because its most distinguishing characteristics were earnestness and temperateness, the speech had been an eloquent deliverance for the Arabs.

It was a bit different for the Zionists as they pleaded for a Balfour Declaration settlement - an agreement that would be honorable to both sides. Both sides are the British and the Jews, regardless of disasters that would follow any other ready-made scene devoid of Arab consent.

Mark Sykes mentioned that moral and physical force must be at the disposal of whatever authority humanity desires to set up to shield the world from war. But the physical strength of a League of Nations must be at the call of a moral authority higher than The Hague. "If you look at Jerusalem, are there not real forces stronger than any man could imagine – the sound effects of Calvary and Sacrifice. The moral force of Zion and eternal Hope, the moral force of Islam and obedience."

Mark Sykes believed that there would be a series of pilgrimages to Jerusalem after the war, more expensive than that city has ever seen before.

21

We have the seeds, Jew, Muslims, and Christians of the trinity of impulses that all tend Jerusalem-ward. After the war, Jews will go in tens and hundreds of thousands, not as colonists, but as visitors, to see where the little seed of Zionism is being planted. Russians will visit Jerusalem in flood, perhaps to two or three hundred thousand. I can imagine even that the Pope himself might call his children to a Pilgrimage of Repentance, and untold numbers are responding to the call.

I can also imagine the followers of other Christian churches going to Jerusalem-ward. And I can see Islam participating in the pilgrimage. Jerusalem is a lodestar that affects all these people.

After the war, we shall have a civilized regime in Palestine, for I cannot imagine even the Central Powers declaring that there can be no peace in Jerusalem.

The Turk had been there since the days of Selim the Grim (1512-1520), and consequently, there had been at work forces which had been using Jerusalem to foment discord in Christendom, of holding Jewry at arm's length, and promoting war and ill-feeling among all men.
Then Mark Sykes asked:

What of the future? We need not question who is going to be in Jerusalem. It is sufficient to know that the Turk has gone and that Jerusalem is minus a strong positive force for ill.

The war will give the Turkish clique a significant setback in Islam, and that means a spiritual revival in Islam of a nature different from anything we have seen before. The intellectual, spiritual Arab

22

and Indian will play a significant role. Muslims will think more of the Word than of the Sword.

Most talks about Jerusalem represented a problem, lacking in much of modern religious life and experience.

Sir Mark Sykes played no small part in the rise of Zionism. With Amery,[12] Sykes was taught the principles of Zionism by the Chief Rabbi, Dr. Gaster, and reached an understanding with France concerning the Sanjak of Jerusalem.
Zionism arose in the Russian pogroms of the nineteenth century. British statesmen made various proposals for satisfying them – Cyprus and Uganda - before the policy of "a national home in Palestine" was finally settled.

Indeed, the real challenge was when Britain and France overcame their fears of bringing a vast region of the Turkish Empire into their Western atmosphere.

---

[12] Leo Amery was First Lord of the British Admiralty, and Mark Sykes was an Assistant Secretary to the War Cabinet.

Chapter 3. *Emir Feisal ibn al-Hussein ibn Ali al-Hashimi.*

Arabia is the world's largest peninsula, attached through Palestine to Egypt and through Syria to Turkey. The rest of her body floats in the Red Sea, Arabian Sea, and Persia Gulf. A fringe of green land beaded by a few cities surrounds the 500,000 square miles [1.3 million sq km.] of desert forming her heartland. This peninsula has been the homeland of Bedouin and Quraysh Arabs since unrecorded history. It has bred no civilization, but its fecund women for five thousand years spawned an abundance of Semitic Arabs for export to the Sumerian, Akkadian, and Babylonian city-states, infusing strength into these effete civilizations with their barbaric vigor.

But that was many years ago before Islam, Christianity, and Judaism.

Perhaps, in 1914-16 the British's most severe challenge was not the Muslims of Arabia but France. The French were inclined to a policy of colonization, by which they wished to substitute the use of the French language for native tongues and make the people into Frenchmen, a dream that had nothing to do with Sykes-Picot. Against this reason, there was another challenge: Emir Feisal (Feisul), "The Arab Prince who the British recommended being the head of the new United Arab Syrian State."

Feisal knew that the Syrians wished to preserve the Arabic language and retain their separateness. For this reason, the Emir was, indeed, the promising King of Syria and Chieftain of the Levant.[13]

---

[13] Here, the Term: *the Levant* includes present days' Egypt, Iraq, Israel, Jordan, Lebanon, Palestine, and Syria.

Emir Feisal bin Hussein bin Ali al-Hashimi was a real Arab gentleman. He loved to see his cohorts, the British gentlemen, win the war. His trust in Mark Sykes was limitless, and his faith in another gentleman – Lawrence – was equally unparalleled.

According to the Sykes-Picot dotted lines drawn during the British push toward Mesopotamia in November 1915, and north of the Arabian Peninsula, there lay a high interior mass of Turkish territory still not disposed of, including the critical cities of Damascus, Homs, and Aleppo. This area was sentenced to some "Arab State or Confederation of Arab States," with which France and England were to come to an *understanding later.* But, by tribal and clannish affiliations, this territory was also divided into zones of influence in which respective powers should have "priority right" and "be the only ones to furnish foreign advisers and officials."

There remained Palestine, and this was set aside also for a *future* agreement.

On the roadmaps of Sykes-Picot, France was to move freely within all the relevant coast of Syria on the Mediterranean as far south as Akka, and all the ports – except that Alexandretta was to be free to British trade. France also got a vast hinterland – a veritable principality - reaching as far as the Tigris River.

The French argued that England was basing her policy on two grounds. One was that Russia had been in turmoil, which the French did not admit to being relevant at all to the Sykes-Picot "Treaty" – *Treaty* was the terminology that the French had been using.

The other ground is that Great Britain and the British armies of hybrid troops conquered Mesopotamia and won all the other victories in Asia Minor with practically no assistance.

And that was true because France had had at most only 5,000 troops there. But, for the French politicians, that small number of soldiers did not invalidate the "Sykes-Picot *Treaty.*"

Some roadmaps - 'dotted lines' - mentioned that the French armies of hybrid troops were to be present in the vast territory bounded by a line starting at Homs (Syria), on the coast, and running northeasterly to Sivas (Turkey) - 436 Miles. Thence through Kharpout and Diyarbakir – 98 Miles, and on the east to the Persian border, thence back southwesterly to a point on the Mediterranean Coast to Syria, just north of Akka.

The Syrian Coast with the hinterland as far back as the desert and as far south as Aintab was under a direct French administration. The rest of the 'dotted line allotment' was to be under French supervision.

When the question of Mandates first attracted attention, France expressed willingness to surrender the northern triangular section of her Sykes-Picot maps ending in an apex at Sivas [in central Turkey]. France argued that that portion formed a big wedge in the territory, which France hoped the United States would take as an Armenian mandate.

Also, France hadn't got the workforce and the firepower to have full control – Mandate - over such a vast region.

Also, the growing revolt, promoted initially by Arab Nationalists, thoroughly sincere, but purely urban, had been aided by an active religious agitation, by propagandists from Syria, and by commanding chiefs of clans who stood to gain by the revival of anarchy prevalent after the Turks began to withdraw.

Now, for the French, what mattered was having a hinterland with access to the sea. Without access to the sea, there would be no use of any backcountry, no matter what. By contrast, what purpose was Beirut to the French without the hinterland - Damascus?

And of what use would Damascus be to Feisal without Beirut?

Consequently, a situation had developed in which Feisal had found himself at swords' points with the French, whom he initially disliked. The French were at swords' points with Feisal, and both were at swords' ends with the British.

At present, Feisal and the French have had one standard contestant – the British. But their shared reticence for the British was thinly camouflaged. The French glossed over the situation because, politically, the so-called Entente Cordiale was still in vigor. Feisal glossed over his disillusionment but could not refuse the British; England subsidized his government and maintained his armies.

"These British and Indian soldiers, so clean and so cheerful, have carried a wonderful load through this campaign. They have borne heat, vermin, mosquitoes, fever, double duty, heavy casualties in the field. Sunstroke, heatstroke, malaria, and typhoid have exacted a grim toll, and anyone who counts the injuries in the various actions, and compares them with the numbers engaged, will perceive that the fighting has in Mesopotamia been as severe, if not as persistent, as anywhere in the war." That was Sir Mark Sykes' account of the *circumstances and difficulties* published in Monday's daily papers on November 15, 1915.

Emir Feisal never thought of any secret agreement being 'cooked' between the French and the British behind his back. Even if his Intelligence officers had dared mention such a matter to him, he would have refuted the news as nefarious and intending to drive a wedge between Arabs and British. He trusted the straightforwardness of the British – Anglo-Saxon – and never had a blink of his thought that any agreement with the 'gentleman,' even by word of mouth, would ever be broken.

Feisal and Mark were like comparing equal with equal. But the Emir's views on the French were something else.

He tried to avoid them like the plague.

He loved to see them out of the Levant and Arabia. When any Frenchman spoke to him through an authorized interpreter, he shut the door to prevent the Frenchman from being heard.

The close of 400 years of Ottoman rule in Damascus came on September 30, 1918, when the Turks were driven out. The next day, a young British archaeologist named Thomas Edward Lawrence – Lawrence of Arabia – whom the British had assigned to join forces with the Arabs under Emir Feisal - entered Damascus.

Two days later, Emir Feisal, atop a beautiful Arabian horse and followed by 1,500 Arab horsemen, made a triumphant entry into Damascus, where an Arab government was set up. Meanwhile, the British commander of the Egyptian Expeditionary Forces, Sir Edmund Allenby, raced to Damascus to assert the 'principles' of Sykes-Picot.
Sykes-Picot!
What principles?
It was the Arabs' first direct encounter with the realities of the Allied hold over Syria.
Indeed, before Feisal's *triumphant entry* into Damascus, a lot of things had happened.
Allenby, as a military man – he was a Field Marshal - was concerned with the application of security within the latest dotted lines laid down on available field maps. The lines and colored zones on the roadmaps agreed upon by Mark Sykes and Georges Picot were modified most of the time per the advancing Allied Forces and under the pressure of events. No one had anticipated that such dotted lines would, in the final analysis, be labeled by the French "a Sykes-Picot *Treaty.*" Such a *'military instrument'* France regarded as a *political* one or a roadmap to thrash out sharp political differences between the Allies themselves.
Several conflicts had already remained unsettled since Napoleon Bonaparte had set his boots in this region, about 120 years before. But this time, Sykes-Picot has had nothing to do with any political and administrative distribution of lands. It began with the recovery and restitution of grounds, with an air of great military

satisfaction, and continued with political derision that the authors – Sykes and Picot – never intended it to be a source of embarrassment.

The roadmaps included documents of understanding to streamline communication between the advancing forces of France and England.

Syria, before the First World War, was part of the Ottoman Empire. After the war, already the dynamics of Sykes-Picot had ended with the end of military hostilities between the coalition of Germany-Turkey, and the British-French armies of mongrel troops of the Muslim faith, mainly from North Africa (France) and India (Britain).

Russia had been privy to the Sykes-Picot saga. The Czar of Russia witnessed how the Allies' military progresses had been achieved by those maps. But revolution soon brought in the Bolsheviks. Unsympathetic to the Allies' cause, they publicly revealed the *Secret Treaty's text*, as they termed it. The stunned Arabs eventually were appeased by the Allies, and they continued to fight to the end.

When the armistice with Turkey was signed in October 1918, the military concentration in Syria was British. Britain at once began paying off her war commitment by dividing Syria into three parts *for civil administration.*

The Syrian coast and much of Lebanon goes to the French administration.

Central and Southern Mesopotamia around the Baghdad and Basra provinces go under British administration. Palestine would have an international authority that the British would oversee.

The division had nothing to do with the dotted lines of Sykes-Picot because those lines had now become stale from a military viewpoint.

Now the guns fell silent; politics should talk.

The rest of the territory – a vast area including modern-day Syria, Mosul in northern Iraq, and Jordan - would have a local Arab Emir under French supervision in the north and British in the South.

The fighting with firepower had become a new kind of war. Now it is a political *fight* in which everyone shoots from the lip.

The French felt betrayed; they wanted more in the hinterland up to Damascus and Latakia. But Emir Feisal, an Arab from the Hijaz in the Arabian Peninsula, had already got an understanding from the British, dating from 1916. This one had nothing to do with Sykes-Picot, either.

At great trouble, the understanding with Emir Feisal had everything to do with the McMahon–Hussein Correspondence, which considers the emergence of Arab nationalism. At that time, the British worked on using 'Arab nationalism' to their advantage against the Turks.

The 'McMahon-Hussein Correspondence' was a series of ten letters exchanged from July 14, 1915, to March 10, 1916, between Feisal's father, Hussein bin Ali, Sharif of Mecca, and Sir Henry McMahon.[14] Perhaps the exchange of letters with a high-ranking British officer was one of the methods England had initially used to "buy time," trying to stir an active Arab Revolt against the Ottoman Empire.

The French, however, got their share through a secret treaty (not Sykes-Picot) signed with the British in 1916, which had been updated within the spirit of the *Entente Cordiale*.[15] France's share foreshadowed the division of Syria, which the Peace Conference was later to approve.

---

[14] McMahon was Britain's High Commissioner in Cairo during the war.

[15] Entente Cordiale is the understanding between Great Britain and France reached in 1904, forming the basis of Anglo-French cooperation in World War I. The Entente Cordiale has never been cancelled or superseded by Mark Sykes and Georges Picot; on the contrary, both were acting within its spirit.

There, the British had picked off Palestine and the Mediterranean Coast, including the Port of Haifa. The French had selected the section of Syria north of Palestine, and the Arabs had pulled off the part north of Palestine.

But it did not go without a diplomatic quarrel.

What happened later was highly anticipated.

French and Arab claims came into direct conflict.

Some Arabs wanted Arab Unity. Indeed, the former period (before the war) always distinguished itself by depression and panic. But the latter period distinguished itself by excitement and wild speculation, both equally unsettling and endangering the Allies' relationship. To avoid a direct clash, the French had been *temporarily* awarded the North-East portion of Palestine, which the Turks had never assigned to a massive Jewish presence.

Those French portions had been changing along with the fighting's progress, and there were no final borders if the fight was going on.

The dotted lines were flexible. For instance, Mosul had been in a peculiar position. The total forces in Mosul were one-eighth of the entire Mesopotamia. Sykes-Picot would have involved a garrison of seven-eighths, at any rate, of the present regiment. Hence, Britain thought it essential to the proper administration of Mesopotamia that the vilayet of Mosul should be part of it. Therefore, they added Mosul to Mesopotamia, which raised debates in the French Parliament, where the French Government had been attacked because they had handed over Mosul to the British *sphere of influence.*

By the dotted lines of Sykes-Picot, the British armies were to be present in Mesopotamia with Baghdad, plus the sea-port of Akka and Haifa, just south of the French line where it reached the Syrian Coast. England got the "direct administration" only of the Mediterranean ports of Akka and Haifa. The "direct administration" also meant 'mandates' in British terminology. England also got a portion of Mesopotamia, between Baghdad and the Persian Gulf – a tiny bit of territory with significant riches in oil and agricultural land when irrigated.

During the war, when Feisal got to Akka, he had to change over and go northward because, subsequently, the British troops were well-garrisoned in Akka. He was now about to invade Syria; he had to send back to the Hijaz every man who had helped him hitherto and to enroll the Syrian tribes and the Syrian villagers in their place.

The Syrian hinterland had been a thorny problem, stretching back to the Euphrates and the Tigris, including Mosul and Diarbekr, with the dear oil and mineral lands adjacent.

So thoroughly did Feisal do this that there were only four Meccans in his Army by the time it reached Damascus. Feisal increased his regulars from 2,000 to 8,000, and these were all men of Syrian or Mesopotamian origin. He raised 20,000 Arabs from the Syrian desert to cover his flank and his communications. When he called for the *levée en masse* and moved to Damascus and Aleppo, he had nearly 30,000 of the proletariat under his banner.

His problem was to unite the tribes against the Turks. That was quite difficult – more so was to make nomad and peasant work side by side against the Turks.

Feisal did it and carried over so much of the war enthusiasm into the peace that his administration maintained public security throughout 1919 and 1920, along with the desert edge of Syria, to a degree never attained by the Turks.

Of course, this standard that lasted about three years[16] in Syria was comparative only, and Feisal's Government

---

[16] Feisal had been "Emir and then King of Syria" for about three years; his reign ended on July 24, 1920, when a French Mandate abolished the Monarchy. Feisal went to Baghdad and named King of Iraq as of

was emphatically a constitutional Government run by Syrians for Syrians – needy, informal, longsuffering. But he was the ruler of a country broken by four years of war, deprived of customs' duties by the terms agreed upon by Mark Sykes and Georges Picot.[17]

Those conditions were changing along with the shifts in the war fields. Also, Feisal was distracted by his Turkish, French, British, and even Jewish neighbors' activities and forbidden all foreigners' advice or technical assistance.

Feisal was perturbed and what disturbed him more than anything else was the absence of mutual understanding between the French and the British on civil matters.

Given the circumstances, it was a miracle that the Emir could last so long.

The dissatisfaction of Feisal's followers with him had always been directed against his moderation. His Western education and his diplomatic experience in Constantinople and Paris had given him broader perspectives than most Arabs. He had no prejudice for or against any Arab province. He was not Meccan nor Damascene nor Mesopotamian nor Egyptian.

He was every bit of those - a cosmopolitan - and a moderate Sunni of the Muslim faith.

Feisal was the pride of the Muslims and the Christians, and the Oriental Jews. He looked upon them all from the platform of his knowledge.

For instance, during the war in Hijaz, Arabs ranted about his permitting the English to enter his area – he told them it was necessary but not dishonorable. The British troops were made up of Muslim Indians whose boots could walk on the Muslim lands without unnecessary ado.

In Akaba, his officers complained that his dependency on Allenby's initiative was wasting the great opportunities

---

August 23, 1921, until September 8, 1933.

[17] Customs duties represent more than half the revenue of the state.

the Arabs held on the flank and rear of the Turks. Feisal replied that the victory would be a team win and that it was only by being a subordinate part of the great machine that they could justify their efforts.

Allenby had been worried about keeping the "dotted lines" as flexible and variable as needed.

Feisal struggled to avoid any quarrels between the Shias and the Sunnis. The feud has many sides, but the thorny one is over the ethical standing of descendants of the Prophet Mohamed.

The Shia mourn individual cruel historical events while the Sunni rejoice and accept them. All Feisal was after is Sunnis of the desert have some slight measure of religious tolerance.

Feisal's troops struck two or three times to force him to take the near and profitable course. He regained their allegiance each time without letting go of a hair of what was essential to Allenby. His father protested that he was neglecting the Meccan point of view – Feisal nearly broke with him before he got the freedom to go Allenby's way. After the victory, Allenby asked him to relinquish much of the ground he had occupied because he wanted to put it under French officers' control, according to the latest and most recent 'dotted lines on the roadmaps' in front of him. Feisal took his word that the arrangement did not prejudice the broader Peace settlement and withdrew his officers at the significant loss of personal prestige.

Then, for tactical reasons, the British evacuated some parts in Arabia, and the Arabs clamored for instant action against the French in alliance with Mustafa Kemal of Turkey. Feisal refused to treat the Turks separately and declined to attack the French, though the French had few men, and Feisal's success was guaranteed.

The British in Mesopotamia fell out with the Arabs, who appealed to Feisal. He transmitted news of their appeal and begged Great Britain to do something to restore contentment of Britain's sphere, and meanwhile, he could keep his 'hot-heads' from troubling the British and gain Britain some time.

The Arabs of Palestine appealed to him for countenance, or even get some help to forestall the Jews. He told them that Zionism was not incompatible with Arab aspirations and stopped his people from taking an active part against the British.

Each such effort to maintain peace and solidarity with his allies cost Feisal adherents. Gradually the extremists fell away from him. He was always attacked for things he had not done, and he had no resources to meet the attacks.

The Syrians called him pro-French, the French called him pro-British. The British called him pro-Arab. The last was the name he would have chosen for himself, but he always protested in public that the Arabs had justified their cause and earned their freedom in the fighting they had done.

The Powers had promised them their independence twenty times and believed that it was ultimately granted by constitutional means.

Emir Feisal deprecated all further attacks against Turks, French, British, Jews, or Christians. He never threatened. When he received notes from the Powers, he invariably referred to the *dotted lines* on his roadmaps.

Aso Feisal, full of character, recalled the British Government's promises to his father and Baghdad's people and the Anglo-French declaration of 1918.

Through the vicissitudes of political misfortune and military fortune, the needle of its compass pointed against him. He felt it was somewhat ironic that his downfall came from the very force he had promised not to use.

When he left the throne of Syria in July 1920, Feisal found himself a free-man with unrivaled experience, excellent knowledge of war and government, the reputation of the most significant Arab leader since

Saladin, and the prestige of three victorious campaigns behind him. He was 35 years of age.

Arab Unions, brought about even by violence, or, as the example of the Kingdoms of Saudi Arabia and Iraq experience showed, by the sword, were to be formed all of a sudden. An utterly new direction was given to the exertions of European politicians. Domestic or economic improvements were neglected for the formation of new political power.

The just end of all legislation, the people's welfare, was disregarded, and an excellent means that might or might not be conducive to that end engaged all attention.

Feisal could not resist the fact that nothing would serve the people but a powerful political instrument – Mandates – though it was more likely to crush and kill the Mandates than save and help.

Later, for this bitter Mandate error, the fallacy that Sykes-Picot had been *an* instrument initially "intended to divide the Levant and Arabia," as claimed by the Arabs, gave expression to some hoarded resentment in London, which astonished all Europe, and America.

Feisal's ambitions for himself had been nothing.

He was the most democratic of men and was gifted with the most charming personality. Still, he had put all his abilities and strength at the Arab National Movement's service for ten years and raised it from an academic question to Western Asia's principal factor.

Undoubtedly the thing that irritated him most was Arab vs. Arab semantics that sapped much of his energy and weakened the Arab National Movement.

At that time, he had seen only roadmaps presented to him by Captain Thomas Edward Lawrence.

Chapter 4. *The Correspondence.*

During the war, the Allied Powers - Russia, France, and Great Britain, came to an understanding of the Turkish Empire's division, in the case of their victory, into 'zones' and 'zones of influence.'

Without knowing, the two battle-field players' - Mark Sykes and Georges Picot – military roadmaps inspired the politicians who exchanged correspondence "printed for the British War Cabinet in April 1917."

The correspondence is non-committal and has nothing to add other than accepting a *fait-accompli* dictated by war conditions.

In other words, the force of events on the battlefield preceded any decision-making of political dimensions. Here is a perfect example of the military *circumstances and difficulties* unduly pressing the politicians on matters that deserve their fullest attention.

All right-thinking men and women will agree that the correspondence gave the armies a touch of political backing to streamline their works based on zones (in dotted lines and different colors).

In these zones, the troops of the three powers – France, England, and the German-Turks' alliance - had been advancing, one against the other.

The primary purpose of such political backing was to avoid the Allies' officers and lieutenants finding themselves pinned down not only by the absence of political cover as the war progressed but by a steady stream of 'friendly fire.' 'Friendly fires' between France and England was possible, notably when the battles are conducted on vast battlefields amid massive political discrepancies.

The British Archives provide a rich cache of letters between Russia and France, notably, about "the Arab Question." The messages[18] were exchanged between countries' officials, France's Ambassador to Russia, Maurice Paleologue, and Russia's Foreign Minister Sergey Sazonov (Sasonoff). But the main ones are those shown in entirety in ANNEX I signed by Britain's Secretary of State for Foreign Affairs, Sir Edward Grey to Paul Cambon, spanning the month of May 1916, then one in August another in October 1916. Grey was later, in December 1916, succeeded by Arthur Balfour.

At that time, Grey challenged Prussia and accused her of advancing for "a Europe modeled and ruled by Prussia. If this were the case, peace would be out of the question." Edward Grey mentioned he had found evidence in the German military philosophy that war and force were the right means of settling disputes between nations.

At that time, the war in France had at last taken a favorable turn.

Hence France took a firm stand that anything said about the duration of the war was unnecessary.

What's necessary was the "fight to a finish."

France believed that the German army's defeat and retreat would bring peace to a military and political sense.

The treaty signed on September 5, 1914, by Sir Edward Grey and Paul Cambon, and Count Benckendorff, the Russian Plenipotentiary, may retard the ultimate settlement. It might well be that terms satisfactory to two of the Allies would be unacceptable to the third.

But the real challenge was not the Russians.
It was the Arabs.

---

[18] By courtesy of the British Archives: Refer to ANNEX I at the end of the book (Catalogue CAB/24/9 Image Ref. 0071) Printed for the War Office – April 1917.

Turkey, being a close ally of Austria and Germany, the news spread in mid-August mentioned that Turkish troops' transport on a grand scale to the European war field was proceeding

> "without a hitch. The troops are being taken from Asiatic provinces of Turkey and also include some Arabs."

In this correspondence, most French and the British feared their association with the Arabs because many Arabs were fighting Arabs on silly disputes.

Most of the time, Inter-Arab relations were not working, except when the Turks oppressed a denomination on account of the other sect – in a divide and rule fashion. There were many classes of Arabs.

One was those in the Levant, of people of a high educational standard.

The others were those residing in the desert.

And a third living in Egypt under the occupation of Great Britain for the last 34 years.

A fourth were those of North Africa of Berber and Sudanese descent.

The cultural differences were appalling. And the legend "Arab Nationalism" was mainly upheld by city dwellers, of the Arab bourgeoisie, not villagers and tent dwellers, or herd-tenders.

Arab Nationalism calls that the unity of Syria is preserved by the warm feelings of Syria's people.

Arab Nationalism calls that whatever foreign administration – whether of one or more power – is brought into Syria, should come in, not at all as a colonizing power in the old sense of that term, but as a mandatory, with the clear consciousness that the wellbeing of the Syrian people forms for it a sacred trust.

But the showstopper toward a vast Arab Federation remained to be a cultural characteristic and living standard.

For instance, Arab students from the deserts and remote places realized that one of the leading features of the nineteenth and twentieth centuries, such as the democratic ideals, had found full expression in the cities. And in that respect, could the Arabs be justly recognized as congenial in national essence to the spirit that governs Cairo, Alexandria, Beirut, Damascus, and Jerusalem.

Conversely, no intelligent person could fail to see that the Arabs of the desert were utterly different.

Deep inside their conscience, the Arabs of the wilderness were the most philosophical and the most religious.

They shouldered a backlog of burdens from Tartar methods of rule and Turkish tutelage, putting its marks on the clans and their chieftains. Such features were not losing their significance despite the recent nationalist awakening.

The war against the Turks could not but distance the desert dwellers from the human brotherhood, charity, and love of personal freedom.

This situation could readily be ascertained when one consults the French and British archives, without bias and prejudice.

Before the Turks and the Tartar invasions that overthrew the whole fabric of social and state institutions in the Levant and Egypt, none of the clans and desert tribes could be founded and built upon constitutional lines. An equally supreme power reigned over religious matters for all Arabs.

Also, there was a difference in the political approach of the British and the French. Being a monarchy, the former was behaving in an atmosphere of monarchies; France preferred republics. She considered monarchies as something of the past; republics are to the future.

The French and the British feared that if the Arabs succeeded in shaking off the Turks, they would automatically mold their reigns, like the autocratic Turks ruled by power.

There was no possibility of Europeanizing the Arabs under such reformers as Mohamed Abdou and Gamal Eddine al-Afghani.

Still, France and England were adamant about securing quicker progress by adopting the forms of West-European culture.

France (and Italy) was the neighboring state on the Mediterranean Sea. Thus, it was only too natural that infiltration of French (and Italian) culture in "an Arab Federation" took place to a certain extent, notably that Egypt was ready to accept French (and Italian) methods more readily than those of the British occupiers.

Such an assumption meant that the Arab Confederation would have to be a Republic, France being a republic herself.

But a single Arab State would not be possible because the crossbreed between the nomads and the city dwellers is considered a heterogeneous element in Arab life. A dream of Pan-Arabism might not enjoy popularity.

In the French's eyes, the Arab bourgeoisie was likened to feudal relics, a plutocracy of the past – this bastard of the aristocracy.

But the British had something else about which to worry. It was the method of grouping the warring nomads and clans to protect Britain's back during the war and Britain's interests.

Discussing the French's concerns of losing in politics, everything they gained in the battlefields prompted the need for shaded areas of military operations that they and the British had to determine.

For instance, during the war, Britain had no problem recruiting 500 troops, from Palestine, for the Hijaz army, of which 200 had been enrolled at Hebron. Palestine was set to be part of the French sphere of influence. When the

British recruited the troops, it was like the British playing in the French court.

Tribal news from Mesopotamia was quite discouraging. Here is an excerpt from the British Archives on the Eastern Report[19] that addresses the period under review and demonstrates the difficulties Mark Sykes and Georges Picot met with setting appropriate and viable colors and dotted lines on their military roadmaps operations.

> *Tribal News.* - In the Mesopotamia report for May, recently received by the British army from the India Office, the following information regarding the local tribes is included: —
>
> 1. The Sinjabis, who had, despite promises, continued their connection with the enemy *(Germany)* have been split up and thoroughly looted by the Kalkhanis and Kalhurs supported by a column of British troops. Ali Akbar is a fugitive, and it is unlikely that he will give any further trouble.
>
> Abdul Karim, son of Fatah Bey and nephew of Mahmud Pasha, who has hitherto shown himself pro-German and pro-Turk, is now thoroughly frightened and wishes to make peace with the British forces.
>
> Shaykh Wahhab, son of Shaykh Hamud, of the Talabani Kurds, has now come in the open to the British and has promised to bring something like 100 horses of cultivators on to his lands at Sanj Bulaq.

---

[19] Excerpts from: Ref CAB/24/125 Image Reference: 0024. (September 5, 1918)

2. A Shabanah post was recently established on the Fallujah road at the Bani Tamim's Shaykhs' definite recommendation. The Shabanah was enlisted from the tribe following the Shaykhs' selection.

No sooner had they received their arms than they held up and robbed a caravan of small merchants on their way from Fallujah to Baghdad, wounding the caravan leader. The crime is serious and is being severely dealt with.

3. The delimitation of the boundary between the Zoba and the Bani Tamim has been carried out by the assistant political officers of Fallujah and Kadhimain. It has long been a cause of bitter hostility between the two tribes. [...]

It appears from the papers captured at Anah from Lieutenant Preusser that Ali Sulaiman, the leading Shaykh of the Dulaim, has written once or twice to the German agent since the occupation of Rammadi.

Still, there is no indication of espionage or actual help given by him to the enemy. He has, on the contrary, been useful to us in intercepting enemy caravans. Still, he has never concealed his anxiety lest we should one day leave him to the mercy of the Turks, and his letters are no doubt due to the wish to provide himself with a means of excuse in that extremity. [...]

As concerns the Russians, most of the dotted lines involving Armenia and Mesopotamia were drawn in yellow. This color does not stick long on yellow papers. Sykes and Picot intentionally did it for two reasons.

The first: Few people at home knew these regions in Yellow.

Even the names mentioned meant nothing to them, while the most terrible and extensive war was being waged in such well-known areas as Belgium, France, North Italy, and Macedonia. Less information was available of the eastern campaigns like Mesopotamia and Armenia.

The second: Mark Sykes and George Picot anticipated that the government of Saint Petersburg would not last. Hence the fear of a revolution.

The question asked was, what about Americas' position? Where are they in all the 'whippings' that filled the post-war scenes?

Without America, the Allies would not have achieved much!

American missionaries had interjected the name of President Wilson, who was said to be lurking around, as his army was still holding "a gun in his lap," fearless of noting.

America, having been on the sideline at the turn of the twentieth century, her media found in Islam a democratic spirit more genuine than any other institution in, for instance, Russia.

But the Allied Powers had different concerns during the war

Chapter 5. *Arabs vs. Arabs.*

So far as Akka, Feisal's forces had been Bedouins, and he had cared to keep the tribes at peace with everyone except the Turks.

Feisal's task had been challenging because he had to group, per the dotted-lines of Sykes-Picot's roadmaps, scores of tribes, chieftains, families, clans, and warlords that had always been vying against one another.

He had heard about the debacles within the Arab Tribes, the Sinjabis' allegiance to Germany, the looting by the Kalkhanis, and Kalhurs. The fugitive Ali Akbar. The pro-Germans and pro-Turks Abdul Karim, son of Fatah Bey and nephew of Mahmud Pasha. The Wahhabis, the Talabani Kurds, the Bani Tamim, the Shabana, and a lot more.

Most Arab tribes have been at war for more than a century. If there had to be a war somewhere, the interior of Arabia was perhaps the least objectionable theater for a war that could be found in the world. Later, and in support of this opinion, which had prevailed during the World War, the British could call, anytime, the evidence of their Foreign Office and the India Office, established in London. The offices vyed one another by proxy in Arabia during the Peace Conference – each arming its Arab champion at the same tax-payers' expense.

The two offices witnessed how, during the War, unconquered clans gave and asked for more lands.

Lately, determined efforts for peace were made possible through Mark Sykes and Georges Picot, something the Ottomans had failed to do peacefully but succeeded by using the whip.

Few people outside individual zones in Arabia could travel from one-quarter to another without being pillaged, and if lucky, remained in one piece.

In the Arab-speaking world and the Levant, those tribes already knew their regions of influence. If ever recognized by an international community, groups of clans united on tribal affiliations would have made at least 80 separate states spanning an average surface area of 160 thousand square kilometers (61,776 Sq. Miles) each.

The dotted lines of Sykes-Picot roadmaps were also trying to group the interrelated clans within large areas rather than dividing them. It attempted to bring together what had already been separated due to creed, individual greed, and nomadism, all looking for fertile lands.

For instance, Egypt's frontiers alongside the Mediterranean Sea erupted suddenly like a volcano in addition to Mesopotamia's troubles.

For some time (about mid-February 1916), signs came out that all is not well in the camp of the Arabs cooperating against the British on the western frontiers of Egypt. The western boundaries extend beyond Alexandria and Mersa Matruh, adjacent to Hazalin-Bir-Shola – Libya (25 miles southwest of Mersa Matruh.) The truce existed for the last few months between the Tripolitan Arabs and some dwellers on the east. This peace came about to the surprise of many who knew the habitual irreconcilable feelings between the tribes concerned. However, the truce ended, owing mainly to the behavior of the Tripolitan Arabs to the Bedouin.

This time it was Arab fighting Arab; clans of Arab descent with Arab culture fighting clans of Arab origin but with a different culture. All of them were Sunni Muslims. Some of the attacks led to hand-to-hand fighting in which a lot were killed. The combat areas were overlapping, and there had been rifle fire along with intermixed spots that a fighter could not recognize a friend from an enemy except through the Arab slang of prisoners.

In the Libyan frontiers with Egypt, thousands of Libyans were seen fighting without even rifles. Some were using spears, clubs, and some throwing stones. All went into the conflicts as fearlessly and as determined as if equipped with the modern British army gear.

With poor tactical organization and with ever-poorer field division, the Arabs, nevertheless, were not able to make a strong case for "Arab unity in one State."

Groups of local Bedouin, fleeing from the Tripolitan Arabs who had arrived in Mersa Matruh, reported that the long-standing friction between the Arabs of the Eastern hinterland and Western Arabs has now reawakened and that an open revolt has broken out owing to the maltreatment of the Bedouins.

A Petition, signed by five Sheikhs of one of the Aulad (sons) Ali Tribes, was brought into Mersa Matruh appealing for protection from the Egyptian Government against their hereditary Arab enemies. The signatories stated that Ahmed Sherif - Grand Sheikh of the Senussi, had been petitioned by the Aulad Ali tribes. They protested against their treatment, which was declared due to Turkish officers, who incited the Tripolitan Arabs to maltreat their Egyptian neighbors and temporary allies.

The condition of the refugees coming in was pitiable.

Some cooperated against the British but deserted in disgust. Others had been hitherto prevented from coming in by the 'Western Arabs,' who deprived them of food and ill-treated them and their families. Some of the victims were even executed for petty disputes. The refugees described the terrible conditions of their comrades, "like hell on earth."

It appeared that the Turkish officers had incited the Tripolitans to make the Aulad Ali bear the brunt of the attacks, and the refugees complained not only of their harsh daily treatment but of the proportionately more

47

massive losses they had been forced to sustain. These things have shown the sub-tribes of the Aulad Ali their fatal mistakes in joining the Tripolitans and convinced them that they had been made merely a stalking horse for Turkish intriguers.

The Aulad Ali, literally the descendants of Ali, is a collection of Bedouin tribes predominating on the Tripoli frontier's Egyptian side.

At the outset of the Senussi aggression, a certain number of the Aulad Ali, together with the neighboring tribes' members, went to the Tripolitan Arabs. These who had now revolted and were coming in. Refugees and Bedouin situated east of Mersa Matruh, who had not shown signs of following their fellow tribesmen's example and joining the enemy, were being accommodated in particular areas in the Hammam district. There, the military authorities were supervising an encampment and market for the supply of their needs.

The Hammam District or Ain El-Hammam is a district in Tizi Ouzo Province in Algeria.

There were significant dangers in building up local militias. They might become a tool of a tribal faction or local warlord. Each tribal faction declared the reconciled ones of their tribe to be traitors and treated them accordingly. For this reason, it was darn tricky for Sykes and Picot to draw meaningful and viable roadmaps. Both had to receive the claims of any tribe and grant it individual sections of land of the territory in dispute; failing this would endanger the Allies' armies' backs.

Chapter 6. *Syria Remains Defiant.*

There were few Turks in Damascus outside of the Turkish government officials. The native Arab population only countenanced their presence because there were not enough Syria arms to end the Turks. Syria had gained freedom from the Turkish government because of the war, but whether she had jumped out of the frying pan into the fire remained to be seen.

The Syrian population was founded upon Arab stock, but significant admixtures of different blood had created a "mixed" type in Syria.

Insofar as the Syrian is an Arab, however, he is an urban Arab and quite distinct from the Arab of the desert – the Meccan officers.

A Syrian Arab knows world affairs.

A Syrian Arab is an excellent businessman, and he has been about the world a bit.

Since his boyhood, Mark Sykes, who had traveled to this region, knew the matter's straight facts. They were that the British Government made a colossal blunder when they plunged into the Levant as saviors from the Turks, to find themselves facing the political 'music' – clannish music and family semantics.

In his analysis of Asia Minor, mandating Syria by the British or the French would counter his experience and findings.

Early on, Mark Sykes realized that the physical division of any area from the rest of Syria would go very far toward meeting the French program of placing France in control of the Levant.

America's interest in Levantine affairs was reviving in the United States.

According to press reports in Paris, a committee of five prominent American senators was to visit that city at once and take testimony from Mark Sykes as to the present conditions in the Levant.

What happened later was not anticipated.

It was shocking.

On Tuesday, February 18, 1919, The Times of Greater London announced the "Death of Mark Sykes; Soldier, Traveler, and Writer."

> We regret to announce the death in Paris on Sunday of Lieutenant-Colonel Sir Mark Sikes, Bt. M.P. *[at the age of forty]*
>
> Sir Mark Sykes returned to England from the East a fortnight ago and left immediately for the Peace Conference in Paris.
>
> On Monday, February 10, he caught a chill, which developed into influenza, followed by pneumonia. Lady Sykes was herself at present dangerously ill in Paris.
>
> Sir Mark Sykes was born in 1879. The only son of Sir Tatton Sykes, Bt., of Sledmere. He was educated at Beaumont College, the Jesuit School at Monaco, Institute St. Louis, Brussels, and Jesus College, Cambridge. [...]
>
> At the age of 12, he was taken by his father on a journey to Palestine and visited Jerusalem and Damascus. Seven years later, he stayed down for a term from Cambridge to make a second foreign tour and visited Syria, Ararat, the Caucasus, and Batum.[20] This tour was not a casual trip to the

---

[20] The second largest city of Georgia located on the coast of the Black

50

sightseer. Still, it was devoted to a close study of peoples, languages, customs, and the development of that faculty, enabling him to approach local questions and understand social ideas from the native perspective.

The death of Sir Mark Sykes left many open questions open.

What was all about those roadmaps marked with dotted lines and colored zones?

Had the late Mark intended them, with Georges Picot, to be for future political reasons or current military exigencies that will end with the war?
There was no mention that the roadmaps were designed to be used as *policy* instruments. Nor had they been designed for such purposes. French politicians considered any military roadmaps to appear like a Treaty. It was like putting the cart before the horse.

Upon the death of Mark Sykes, Georges Picot felt lost.
He was wandering and wondering about anything to do concerning the times he spent with Mark Sykes. Astonishingly, what he saw on those maps, after the war, were now insignificant.
During the Allies meetings at Versailles, his interpretations of the various plans, and the dotted lines thereon were not flawless, that his French bosses preferred him out of the *'game.'*

By 1919, the Syrian sentiment against the French was so elevated that no peaceful settlement of the Syrian question was possible with a permanent French authority over Syrian soil.

Sea in the country's southwest.

The puzzle was, "What is the solution to the Syrian Question?"

It remained nagging and continued to be an open question! Given the desires of the Syrian natives, and the Anglo-French declarations of 1916 and 1918, it would seem that the only possible solution

> is an American Mandate. This Mandate is the more to be wished; in effect, it would ultimately have on[21] the *Entente Cordiale*. It is widely doubted in Europe at present [1919] whether the United States could refrain in administering a benevolent mandate from playing the old *game*, which just now is threatening the disruption of the *Entente Cordiale* in Syria. It is sincerely doubted whether there can be any basis for international understanding besides the present basis of thievery and chicanery.[22]

But why did the Syrians prefer an American Mandate?[23]
By the middle of 1916, Syria and Lebanon were in a serious plight. And appeals had been made to America for assistance.

All the Holy Land felt the blight of the war.

The shutting off of food imports by the Allied blockade and poor railroad communication, the requisitioning by

---

[21] 'have on' means 'trick or deceive'in the British parlance

[22] In 1904, France (Russia's ally) and Britain (now Japan's ally) faced a quandary. To prevent being dragged into the conflict, the French and British shucked off their ancient rivalry and concluded an *Entente Cordiale* whereby France gave up opposition to British rule in Egypt, and Britain recognized French rights in Morocco.

[23] The British Archives, however, mentioned "In the case of Palestine, for instance, both Jewish and Arab elements in the population were quite definitely in favour *(sic)* of a British and not of an American mandate." Catalogue Reference CAB/23/42 Image Ref 0016, Friday, December 20, 1918 at 11 AM. Palestine was not considered part of Syria.

Turkey of large stocks of food, and a peculiarly disastrous locust plague in the fall of 1915 brought the whole section to the verge of starvation.

In Syria, all 'draft' animals were requisitioned by the Turks.

All non-disabled men were called to fight with the Turkish army, and no one was left to till the fields.

But who did the blockade?

The coast of Syria (and Lebanon) was under blockade by the Allies, and this was working great hardships on the inhabitants of Palestine and Mount Lebanon.

The people believed that an appeal from the Holy Land would inevitably not fall on deaf ears in "Christian America."

It had been asserted that the end of the European war would be followed by dire poverty and, perhaps, by famine in the more significant part of Europe. These assertions had frequently been contradicted by men who maintained that nature repairs the ravages of 'man,' and in the future, nature, as has always done, would provide food – that is, if 'man' was ready to cooperate with nature.

By September 1916, Washington interfered.

The Turkish government agreed to shipments of relief supplies from the United States to famine sufferers only in Syria and Mount Lebanon.

The action reversed Turkish officials' previous attitude, who had refused two urgent pleas by the State Department to make shipments.

The consent of the Ottoman government in Syria did not apply to Armenia.

Distribution of supplies, which already had been offered in generous quantities by Syrian and Armenian Relief Societies, would be made under the Turkish plan through Beirut's port if Turkey agreed.

The French government had been anxious to get such supplies through and might have herself contributed to obtaining the Entente Allies' consent for passage of shipments through the blockade.

The Turkish government took the Americans quite seriously and agreed that Syria's supplies were distributed from Beirut through the Red Cross and Red Crescent Societies, excluding Armenia.

The famine killed thousands.

And thousands more were preparing to leave the region. Words received that the number of Americans seeking to leave Syria and Palestine had grown from a few hundred to more than 2,000. The news caused the State Department to arrange with the Navy for indefinite use of the Cruiser Des Moines and the collier Caesar, to bring the refugees out.

Barcelona, Spain, was the nearest 'neutral' port.

The port had been selected as the place where to land the Americans for trans-shipment home on commercial liners. At least one trip of the Caesar, nearing Beirut with 2,500 tons of relief supplies on board and two visits of the cruiser Des Moines, also on her way to Beirut, was required to 'lift' the refugees.

After protracted negotiations, the Allies permitted both vessels to pass through the blockade with their relief supplies aboard. Turkey agreed to conduct them through the mine zones in the harbor. Most of the refugees were naturalized Syrians, Armenians, and Hebrews. There were also numerous American missionaries, some of whom had been trying for more than a year to get out of the stricken district.

Beirut was the only point of exit opened by the Turks, and as many of the refugees would have to travel a long distance by the most primitive means of conveyance, it was some time before they got to Beirut.

In 1916, conditions in Syria and Palestine had been dreadful, with famine and pestilence on all sides. "The Allies are the modern Mongols, the Americans are the angels," thus spread the words in angel whispers.

Syrian attitude in the matter of the British was more moderate than imagined. The Syrians were under no disillusionment concerning Britain's ambitions.

They knew that a British mandate in Syria was equivalent to handing over the country to England. They prejudged that the British, once established in Syria, would never leave.

The example of Egypt was quite vivid in the memories of the Syrians.

The Syrians respected the British, but they appreciated them for what their long record among backward people showed them to be.

The Syrians resented backwardness far more than they disliked the French.

The Syrians also rejected the Zionist project that the British had wished onto Palestine without consulting them.

Indeed, the Syrians were as opposed to the Zionists as they were to the French. To them, the Zionist movement was an immediate threat to their homes in Palestine. There were not significant portions of Palestine, which were then arable. These parts in 1919 and prior, were settled by Syrian farmers.

The Syrians knew that these lands would be desired for Jewish farmers if the Zionist project was realized, and the result was that the land would be bought out.

Hence, the determination of the Syrians to oppose the Zionist project was easily understandable. *"Great as was the wrong which, a long time ago, the dispersion had inflicted upon the Jewish people, the Zionist project would only right it by committing another mistake upon the native population."*[24]

---

[24] Refer to Naguib Azoury "The Awakening of the Arab Nation," 1905. *Native population* refers to Greater Syria which includes present days' Jordan, Palestine-Israel, Lebanon, and Syria.

Chapter 7. *The King-Crane Commission.*

The British and French persisted in a struggle over the dotted lines' details on the roadmaps, as the Arabs pressed demands for independence.

At the Big Four's meeting on March 20, 1919, Woodrow Wilson proposed that an Inter-Allied Commission visit Syria "to elucidate the state of opinion and the soil to be worked on by any mandatory, and report their findings to the Peace Conference." The Supreme Council adopted Wilson's suggestion. But the French refused to appoint representatives, and, although the British had already named theirs, Whitehall also withdrew. As a result, only the two American members, Henry C. King and Charles R. Crane proceeded to the area with their staff. They arrived at Jaffa on June 10 and filed their report and recommendations with the American delegation in Paris less than forty days later.

The message of sending American envoys to the Levant was a welcome proof that President Wilson's illness had not impaired his clear apprehension or his full and sound judgment of public affairs. Wilson had always been after soliciting "the peoples' opinion about any decisions concerning their future." It's like getting the people to be part of the decision-making process.

The American envoys recommended that Syria becomes a *constitutional monarchy* under Feisal with the necessary US protection.

But the Allies ignored the Commission's report.

Indeed, the USA – respected as a neutral power by the Arabs – retreated into its pre-war isolationism.

Still, there is a lot more than that.

Not only was Wilson's illness a matter of concern, but also the dastardly attempt made on the life of Clemenceau was predominant. After five days of acute anxiety, it was possible now to believe that his life was out of danger to a certain extent.

At the moment, the January 1919 Peace Conference had more or less relapsed into silence; The United States was not bound to honor any pre-existing agreements among the Allied Powers. The fact is that the delegates believed that the work could be proceeded with more rapidity by informal conversations than by a set of meetings of The Council of Ten, which was then the official body.

The economic aspect of the post-war situation was of prime importance and almost eclipsed any other issue.

There was a problem with silly things like whether Germany should hand-over dyes, machine tools, agricultural implements, raw materials, and so forth to France. On the one hand, there was a pack yelping that any such settlements meant dumping the appalling conditions. On the other hand, it was pointed out that unless Germany paid with what she had, the Allies would be left without indemnity or security for compensation. But Germany was almost broke; all she could afford was bits and hardware pieces from here and there.

Instead, would the indemnity be dividing the rich Levant among France and Great Britain and Russia and Italy? And if so, would the voice of the people be considered at all?

It doesn't make any difference how innocent a president like Woodrow Wilson maybe if he gets a case of alterations, he needed right now one of those red-colored *'Exists,'* as they have in hotel hallways.

Initially, the Peace Conference included the *Big* Ten. President Woodrow Wilson and Secretary of State Robert Lansing represented America. Lloyd George, Arthur Belfour, and General Edmund Allenby, the British Empire. Georges Clemenceau, Stephen Pichon, Henri Berthelot, France, and Vittorio Orlando and Sidney

Sonnino, Italy. It was eventually considered a crucial meeting. Wilson returned to America. Before he had gone away, he had two essential things.

After the fierce controversy, he had forced the adoption of the mandatory principles to control the "old empires" and the former German colonies.

Second: He had made (February 1, *Council* of Ten)[25] a blunt declaration of the American attitude toward the old secret treaties, though, at that time, he knew only of a few of them and had no idea of the *vast web* of secret diplomacy yet to be revealed.

> As any of the secret-treaties in question does not bind the United States, the US is quite ready to approve a settlement by facts.[26]

There had been some hard thinking about these pronouncements of Wilson while he was away. What did he mean? How far did he intend to go? For if the Mandatory system were to be sincerely adopted as the world's policy, it inferred a knockout blow to many of the advantages of international spheres of influence in which the *old diplomacy* was so genuinely interested. It meant, for instance, the 'open door.' And for what use was a colonial expansion without financial control of privilege? And a settlement on a 'basis of *fact*?'

The old order wanted *possession*, not facts.

The United States' envoys would let in at once *inquiries*, not of what the Great Powers *wanted for themselves*, in oil, silver, copper, pipelines, but what the people who inhabited all these vast regions, of whom nobody thought

---

[25] The Supreme Council of the 1919 Paris Peace Conference, also known as the Council of Ten, consisted of the five chief representatives of the US, France, United Kingdom, Italy and Japan, each accompanied by his foreign minister.

[26] The British Archives CAB/ 24/85 of June 3, 1919 – Committee of Enquiry, Breaches of The Laws of War.

what they wanted, and how their real welfare was to be secured.

These two principles of Woodrow Wilson, if carried out, would knock out the old diplomacy sky-high and rob the secret treaties of every shred of their importance or value.

Hence, the importance of this meeting on March 20 when the French had put up on the wall of Lloyd George's study a large map of Asiatic Turkey with territories colored to show the secret negotiations' entire history. It was the first occasion that President Wilson had ever heard of the Sykes-Picot (*Treaty* as the French were adamant about mentioning) or of the agreements at St. Jean de Maurienne. Disgusted, President Wilson said of Sykes-Picot, "it sounds like the name of the tea. It is an excellent example of the old diplomacy."[27]

No sooner were these secret agreements made – at the beginning of the war - between the British and the French than Italy became much discontented.

The Italians believed that France and England had had serious plans within the Sykes-Picot roadmaps to allow no other nation any rights in all this significant part of the old Turkish Empire. Italy feared that arrangements had already been made to begin economic development by building a new railroad from Baghdad direct to Aleppo, where England could connect to Alexandretta's sea for her Mesopotamian oil. Undoubtedly, Italy had learned of the general provisions in the roundabout ways known as "the old diplomacy."

The Italians saw that France was getting a much more substantial share in Turkey than Italy under the numerous restricted discussions and London's secret agreements. Almost one year before the March 20 meeting, and by 1918, the Americans felt that secret negotiations had begun. This time including the Italians, and dragged along

---

[27] The British Archives CAB/24/138 of July 3, 1922 attachments to the League of Nations.

during all the year just before the Americans came into the war – April 6, 1917 - and at the very time that Allied political leaders were issuing declarations of charitable war aims.

France and England were playing *volte-face* as "the old diplomacy." They were using the Americans and tried to outsmart them as the French and British armies advanced. And the moment the two nations could make military successes, their primary policies were reversed.

Initially, from London's secret agreements and restricted discussions, France also got a vast hinterland – a veritable principality – reaching east as far as the Tigris River, where her trade could again move freely.

Initially, (as mentioned before), England was content with direct administration of the Mediterranean ports of Akka and Haifa and the portion of Mesopotamia between Baghdad and the Persian Gulf. It was a bit of territory with significant riches in Oil and agricultural land when watered, and these were the field where her armies could move freely.

Between these claims, and north of the Arabian Peninsula lay a high mass of Turkish territory still not disposed of, including Damascus, Homs, and Aleppo's critical cities. This territory was "Arab State or Confederation of Arab States," with which, in their secret talks, France and England were to come to an understanding *later*.

But this territory also was divided into military zones, colored, as appropriate in dotted lines, during the fighting with the Turks, supported by the Germans' proxies. Such ex-battlefields were meant to be split into *areas of influence* in which the respective powers should have "prior rights over local enterprises and loans" and "be the only ones to furnish foreign advisers and officials."

Any other talks about how to penalize Germany would thin-out compared with the treasures that France and Great Britain would be getting out of the Levant and the Arabian Peninsula.

Again, there remained Palestine, and this *was set aside* also for a *future* agreement.

Sykes-Picot did not 'zone' Palestine *per se* because Jerusalem was a taboo.

Later, it became public knowledge that in March 1919, when Wilson suggested the King-Crane Commission, Syria's problem first arose in Paris. Wilson had also appointed the Commission's American members, which was first "accepted in principle" as the diplomats say. Still, he was obstructed and delayed in every way possible, primarily by the French.

Neither France nor England, whose soldiers were in control of Syria, wanted a commission whatever.

Again and again, President Wilson brought up the matter in the Council of Four,[28] but there was always some reason for elbowing it aside.

In the meantime, as can be remembered, Crane and King cooled their heels in Paris, though not without benefit, for Paris at that time housed many representatives of the region under discussion and afforded an excellent opportunity for making preliminary studies of the whole situation.

While the Commission was prepared beforehand for some disinclination toward France in Syria, the strength, universality, and persistence of anti-French feeling among practically all Muslims and non-Catholic Christians - except a division of the Greek Orthodox – came as a distinct surprise to the Americans.

Friends of the French affirmed that the Syrians' negativity toward France was German and Turkish propaganda. They also argued that it was succeeded by Arab and British propaganda and that it was not deep-seated.

Nevertheless, the Commission went to great pains in testing these affirmations by questioning the grassroots – the people. By so doing, they discovered that the anti-

---

[28] The US, Britain, Italy and France. (The Big Four).

French feeling did seem to be deep-rooted in a more substantial proportion of the Syrian population.

The people looked at the French as enemies of religion, having none at home, and supporting Roman Catholics abroad for purely political motives. Another reason: the Syrians "disapprove of the French attitude toward education."

> French education is superficial and inferior. It leads to familiarity with that kind of French literature, which is irreligious and immoral. The Muslims recognize that the time has come for Muslim women's education, and they say that those who receive French training become uncontrollable. The French have also shown a marked tendency to give an undue proportion of offices, concessions, and the like to Syria's Christians. Non-Catholics complain that the same discrimination is indicated for Catholics and Maronites. By such discrimination and various intrigues since the occupation of Syria, the French have increased the religious division in Syria, which had been reduced considerably during the war toward Arab nationalism.[29]

Five months later, by mid-August 1919, there was significant consternation in Aleppo.

The situation there cut deeper than had been indicated. The people had been against a French Mandate. But nobody could understand what they wanted. They were not even accepting its inevitability. Had Britain withdrawn her troops altogether from Syria and French forces to a large number replaced them, then it would have been possible for France to have imposed herself?

---

[29] The British Archives, and The Wilmington Morning Star, September 18, 1922, and other American newspapers.

The British knew that ultimately France would impose herself because she knew the British weakness: the taxpayers.

In London, there was dissatisfaction that the British taxpayer had been paying for no result except to make bad blood with France. But it was indeed uncertain for the French to gather the quality of the troops they would require. Senegalese battalions would not bring peace in Syria, least of all in Aleppo. There was a little *white* artillery regiment, and the automobile corps were small units of Indo-Chinese (Annamites) and Senegalese, the total amount of which, however, hardly surpassed 2,000 men. The number of Senegalese, the only ethnic African troops, amounted to some 1,300. A medley of Senegalese, Algerians, and Moroccans was viewed as men of an *inferior race and culture.*

Questions arose as to whether they were proper individuals to be quartered upon the Arab Syrians and in the house of *white* people.

The French had lost so many men in the war that they could not give needful protection or fair administration. Such a state of affairs was illustrated by the few soldiers and the inferior type of French officers and officials in Syria. It was affirmed that bribery and intrigue were worse in French areas now than under the Turkish rule.

Syria was not a demobilized country like Bulgaria. The Syrian situation was far different than the French had thought. Many fierce soldiers would have to be allocated if the British withdrew, perhaps as many as 100,000. The French General Staff could not find half that number.

But why was such a large number necessary?

The situation was as clear as crystal. It was becoming worse month after month and became an issue between many Muslims and many Christians.

The Maronites quite definitely preferred the French.

This preference was not little gratitude to the memory of Napoleon III when France claimed herself as protector of the Maronites in Lebanon. Nor was it in recognition of the

French schools, culture, and commercial enterprise from which they had benefited, at a time the British were comparatively unknown.

In some villages in central Mount Lebanon, the love between the Maronites and France was mainly for a reason stated more than once by Syrian Christians – namely, that they feel that in ruling the country, the French would more resolutely champion the Christians. In contrast, they believed that the British and the Americans had a weakness for the Muslims.

The Arabs - city dwellers - being allies, were all armed.

If Damascus's hidden stores were opened, there might be 300,000 guns in that one town alone, and a bazaar was full of revolvers for any man to see. And no Arab, from Emir Feisal down, answered but one to the question what they would do: If the French wanted to take Damascus, they must take it by force. If the Arabs were driven out, they would maintain themselves on the Houran flank, and southwards toward the Hijaz, where, doubtless, Palestine, already pinpricked, would suffer from them as noisy neighbors.

Astonishingly enough, it seemed that France did not realize the size of Syria's job and thought it worth doing. The British feared that France might be forced to divide Syria into small areas, leaving the French in Beirut, the Arabs in Damascus, and the British in Jerusalem. Such a solution, in the fall of 1919, was seen as disastrous. And so firmly was the unity of Syria felt that most British staff officers speculated that if the French were to have Syria, they should have Palestine. Also, such a solution, in the fall of 1919, was possible now that the Americans had disgustingly 'withdrawn.'

At that time, there was a danger that the Syrians might try to force the hand of Europe by violent agitation. In Aleppo and Damascus, nerves were strained by a long delay. Mornier, the French Admiral, and his aide-de-camp, who were in a motorcar with Georges Picot, were shot and severely wounded around mid-August. None knew who the culprit was, except it was done "by mistake in a *feu de joie* in their honor."

Was that so?

It must be remembered that Picot's cohort, Mark Sykes, had been dead for about six months. Only everyone knew that the French had had some fighting about Latakia. And might, anytime, become the object of manifestation. Aleppo was placarded with the Young Arab Party's manifestos, written in Arabic and not entirely satisfactory English as "No life witout *(sic)* independence." And "Syria must be undyvayded." To the Arabs, Palestine "is part of Syria." To the Zionists, if France got Palestine, Palestine would remain in Syria. Hence, there were multiple question marks with various characteristics for each.

With all this mishmash, the Americans were not ready to take "crumbs of bread and cake and say, "thank you;' instead, they preferred to wait and see what was going to happen.

No one could understand why Emir Feisal and Clemenceau could not reach an agreement when the former was in Paris. In October 1919, Emir Feisal went to Paris, and toward the end of his visit, Lloyd George urged him strongly to agree personally with Clemenceau.

An interview took place, which resulted in a verbal agreement, of a vague kind, that cooperation between French and Arabs as possible on the basis, per Emir Feisal, of Arab "independence." The Emir returned to Damascus to find a sort of underground war between his people and the French. The interview results had entirely disappeared, and the Emir was entirely in harmony with the anti-French party.

By 1919, there were about 300,000 Syrians in the United States, and many Syrian business houses in Beirut, Tripoli

(Modern Lebanon), and Latakia had branches in New York and St. Louis.

> There has been a steady flow of population from the Syrian-Lebanon to the United States for the last ten years. They still go up unto Lebanon and look at the red-tiled roofs in its numberless villages. The money to build four-fifth of them came from the United States. The funds go into the leading business in Damascus, Aleppo, Beirut, and Jerusalem. Their sons have schooled at the American Protestant College in Beirut. America is a gospel in itself throughout Syria today.[30]

It all came at a time when the United States overtly opposed the pretensions of the Zionists to create a Jewish commonwealth in the southern part of Syria,

> "known as Palestine, and oppose Zionist migration to any part of our country *(US)*, for we do not acknowledge their title, but consider them a great peril to our people from the national economic and political points of view. Our Jewish compatriots shall enjoy our common rights and assume the common responsibilities."[31]

When Emir Feisal argued with Clemenceau and could not convince him to his way of thinking, Feisal described Clemenceau as a very 'hard-headed' French man. Feisal went back to Damascus, convinced his way of thinking showed him a 'very strong-willed' Emir because he refused to ignore the resident people's rights.

---

[30] -Ibid-

[31] The American Archives on King-Crane Report...The Wilmington Morning Star, September 18, 1922.

Chapter 8. *Georges Picot.*

Nine months after Mark Sykes died, Georges Picot became a "lone wolf."

He fed his government with his interpretation of the discussion he had made with Mark Sykes. He did his best to rationalize the dotted-colored-lines on the latest available roadmaps – all vital to France's success in her claims over the Levant - until there was a break between France and England over their different interpretations.

In October 1919, "Who would get what?" was a sordid battle over loot.

All the divine principles France and England subscribed upon America's entry into the war [April 2, 1917] had been disregarded or forgotten. The rights of the resident peoples were ignored. Both powers wanted territory, and each was jealous of the other.

France claimed that its historical rights to Syria went as far back as the Crusades.

Of course, France heeded her political claims, both the commercial advantages that would accrue to her from Syria's possession and the *increased workforce* from Syrian soldiers' conscription into the French army.

On the other hand, England wanted to consolidate her territory to be a solid strip of land over which the British flag would fly from the Mediterranean Sea to China's borders. She already *possessed* Egypt and took *control* of Mesopotamia and Persia, with her power in Afghanistan heightened by the recent war of 1914.

Arabia was under British dominance through her sway over the Holy Cities of Islam and the creation of Hijaz's puppet state.

British soldiers were in Palestine and Syria; Great Britain needed the confirmation of her right to remain there to give her full and undisputed possession of every foot of land from the Mediterranean to Burma's Chinese borders.

If America couldn't be installed as a real buffer power in Armenia, the British would also retain control.

In addition to regional solidarity, Great Britain thus confirmed her immediate possession of the Baghdad Railway. The British secured eastern Turkey's unlimited resources in oil, cotton, wheat, and other products, not to mention the general commercial advantages that would ensue. But *the giant game* concerning international politics between the "big powers" continued with each one unscrupulously seeking to add something to their benefit.

Nevertheless, the American King-Crane Commission's presence had been diverting and disturbing to the French and the British.

It was this Commission that united the two powers on one thing: "get America out."

But Why?

For the first time, the answer is because the King-Crane Commission considered the indigenous people's voice, which should be heard before their fate is decided.

Astonishingly enough, this had been the formally declared principles of the Allies into the Mideast region, where they have been all forgotten.

Astonishingly enough, Georges Picot had been gravely failing in his duty, as a diplomat, toward the people of Lebanon and Syria. In speaking his final words at Paris, he conveyed not the Levantine people's voice, but with the sound of France's naval and military power, based on Senegalese soldiers.

Beirutis have had bad memories of the Turks' oppressive actions due to Picot's lousy performance in 1916.

The story of the French in Beirut begins at the beginning of WWI when Georges Picot, age 46, then French Consul in Beirut, left for France upon the breaking of diplomatic relations, following the Gallipoli Campaign - April 1915 to January 1916 - leaving his secret papers in his safe at the French Consulate.

Six weeks later, the Turks broke into the Consulate, rifled the safe, discovered the names of 25 Syrian[32] secessionists who had been active with the French, and hanged them all on May 6, 1916.

In consequence, the popularity of Picot among the Syrians may be imagined. Adding insult to injury, the French made the crowning error of returning Picot to Beirut as France's High Commissioner upon the city's occupation on October 8, 1918.

Since then, the cost of living had risen enormously in Beirut. Early in the occupation, the Vacuum Oil Company[33] imported a quantity of petroleum into Beirut and began selling it at $0.80 per gallon. The French, who had been selling the same for $1.42, imposed a minimum price of $1.41 immediately on American Petroleum, the cost to be valid if the French supply lasted. On top of the fact that the change from Turkish to the Egyptian *piaster,* which came with the occupation, increased prices by two, it was 1-4 times in Beirut. Also, the French permitted the tramway company to raise its fares seven times. Muslims have had more severe charges than this to bring against France.

> Last Easter Sunday, in 1919, native Christians in Latakia *(Ladkia)* made demonstrations in which they damned the Prophet *(Mohamed)* and carried the Cross into the Mosques. The French have exercised pressure of every sort to bring the Muslims into line. They have even made Friday the official day of rest for government offices in

---

[32] At that time, speaking of Syria also included Beirut and Tripoli, subsequently the capital of present-day Lebanon.

[33] Later in 1955, Mobil Oil Co.

Beirut, even though Beirut's population consists of 110,000 Christians and 40,000 Muslims.[34]

Beirutis loved to hate the French High Commissioner in Beirut, Georges Picot, whose name was a familiar one to natives and foreigners alike throughout Syria.

Many people thought of Georges Picot as an intolerant and capricious weakling. Instead, Picot wanted to prove he was a most gracious and charming and reasonable gentleman. Speaking in a quiet tone and uttering gravest sentiments in a gentle and measured voice. "No interviewer could have a more satisfactory time than I enjoyed with the French High Commissioner," said William T. Ellis, Correspondent of the Minneapolis Tribune and New York Herald on September 29, 1919:

> He *(Picot)* outlined the Syrians' character, now just out of ten centuries of slavery, and the necessity of acquiring western standards of civilization before they can govern themselves. At present, independence is impossible for Syria. Their native life is almost anarchy. In a village where there are four families, three will be fighting against one. Practically, all the people in Syria's eastern divisions want France as suzerain – he could not speak for the east. The idea of a united Syria - with Palestine and the east region, merged with Lebanon - he approves as logical.

[34] Refer to various French Newspapers, excerpts from The British Archives, and Detroit Free Press – Michigan, Sunday, October 12, 1919. Most probably the Archives have mixed between Nusayri and Christians. Nusayri could be misinterpreted as Nusrani i.e. A Christian. In fact, the sect is believed to have been founded by Ibn Nusayri during the Ninth century. For this reason, Alawites are sometimes called "Nusayrism" (*Nuṣayrīyyah*), though this term has come to have derogatory connotations in the modern era; another name, "Ansari" *(al-Anṣāriyyah)*, is believed to be a bad transliteration of "Nusayri." Today, Alawites represent 11 percent of the Syrian population and are a significant minority in Turkey and northern Lebanon.

Does the 'treaty' of 1916 still hold good, despite the 1918 declaration and the Paris Conference platform? Of course, nobody has any other thoughts. It has already been decided in Paris that the Sykes-Picot is possible. [...]

Gorges Picot held his government's view that Sykes-Picot had been a political instrument and not only military roadmaps as the British claimed it to be. But what if the people should ask for Great Britain as mandatory over Syria?

"Then, had there been a break between the two nations, we should have lost the war. The question of good relations between France and England is the most important, and we have sacrificed much for it. But not this." Here his Excellency *(Picot)* spoke sharply and emphatically, "If Syria is not given to France, then the right relations with England snap."

Georges Picot further added that there could be no thought of a single Mandate for all of Turkey.
"It would cost a milliard of the year for the upkeep of troops and administration. When a nation has no interest, you cannot expect it to spend a farthing."
He conceded that to split the land into separate mandates would cost considerable money, but this would be returned to the nation expending it.

"As I left the office of Mr. Picot, it was with a feeling that beneath his unruffled suavity lies an unshakable resolution that Syria shall belong to France and that he is irreconcilable to any other program," said Ellis.

When this interview and necessary declarations were made, Mark Sykes had been dead for about seven and a half months. For this reason, Georges Picot could freely expand on Syria's subject without worrying about somebody telling him he was dreaming strange nightmares.

Many schools of thought argued this: If there had not been a war in 1914-1919; if all the world had not been helpless to start another war; now there would have been one in the present British-French disagreement in the Levant.

At least with all the ingredients of what used to be called "war scare," anything was possible. For instance, the Fashoda incident,[35] or the scramble for Africa, offered nothing by comparison with the present heart-burnings in the French Foreign Office over the British policy in Syria since the war ended.

But this time, there was no 'war scare' over Syria.

Not only 'no war scare' but **Frenchmen** most deeply resentful of the British attitude in Asia Minor and the Levant explored the idea of there ever being another war between England and France.

Even the term "strained relations" was too strong an **expression** to use about the situation, for what strain existed was much more than offset by French gratitude to

---

[35] The Fashoda Incident or Crisis was the climax of imperial territorial disputes between Britain and France in Eastern Africa, occurring in 1898. A French expedition to Fashoda on the White Nile river sought to gain control of the Upper Nile river basin and thereby exclude Britain from the Sudan. The Fashoda Incident, also known as the Fashoda Crisis, was the climatic event caused by years of territorial disputes in Africa, between France and Great Britain. This European obsession with the African continent began in the 1670s, which ended in the partition of the entire continent by 1895. The "Scramble for Africa" is the invasion, occupation, colonization and annexation of African territory by European powers during the period of New Imperialism, between 1881 and 1914. It is also called the Partition of Africa and the Conquest of Africa. The purpose of Sykes-Picot was the avoidance of such scramble, and streamline the areas of military activities between rival, non-European troops acting under the French and British national flags.

72

England for the prompt action of the British Parliament in ratifying the separate treaty to come immediately to French assistance in case of "German aggression."

Still, in her gratitude for this British assurance of protection on the Rhine, France by no means was disregarding the fact that in the opinion of the Quai d'Orsay, England was deliberately violating French rights in a large section of Asia Minor and the Levant.

In November 1919, The New Syrian National League in the USA appealed to Syrian residents in the United States to work for the *American Mandate* over Syria instead of the French mandate.

The Syrians in the USA claimed it as being the desire of most of the Syrian people. The League's program mentioned,

"Syria for the Syrians, independent and undivided under American guardianship," which was hailed with supreme joy in America.

It also said:

Great Britain and France are in sharp disagreement. Neither of these nations can tolerate a general mandate of the other over Syria. Neither of them is trying to preserve the unity of the country. The interest of France in Lebanon is not invested right. A secret treaty between Great Britain and France should not annul the rights of the natives to self-government and self-determination. It should not control America's action or that of the other members of the League of Nations [...][36]

---

[36] The Philadelphia Inquirer, November 5, 1919.

The declaration also mentioned that the unity of Syria and peace could not be maintained if Lebanon could separate, and Lebanon "suicides if she does separate."

France wanted to fall back on Sykes-Picot as proof of her claims in the Levant.

For instance, in Asia Minor, British troops of occupation and British civil administration were kept in control, despite various urgent appeals from the French Foreign Office to have them withdrawn and territory placed in French charge "in line with Sykes-Picot roadmaps."

But the cold English diplomats played the French claims low key and brought no undesirable reaction.

On this news, the World was relieved.

This 'control' of one's nerves meant world peace. Arrangements had to be made at Versailles and in twenty-seven Allied nations; delegations had to come halfway around the world from Japan, China, Australia, South Africa, South America, India.

A month was the period envisaged when the armistice would be signed; the limit of the fulfillment of the terms in every case was fixed at thirty-one days.

Except Greater Lebanon and Palestine were fixed at thirty-six days.

Chapter 9. *Greater Lebanon*

During the peace talks at Versailles, out of the numerous differences in interpretation between France and England, the former mentioned Beirut's case, which was almost at the center of the coastline.

While the railway company monitored by France secured the passenger traffic to the interior, it was also estimated that 10 percent of the imports were carried through Beirut. Both France and Great Britain were beginning to fear the Mandates' burden they had promised themselves to undertake in the Levant.

They would be happy with the mineral and underground resources, but not the people.

They prefer an area without people.

France objected that England was controlling Beirut. A Frenchman might have had business in Beirut before the war. Now he was not permitted to go there. Still, an Englishman, or an Italian, who had no business there before the war now had no difficulty going to Beirut to establish an entirely new enterprise. There was a time in European history when such conditions would indeed have meant war, but happily, there was no danger of that now, as bad as things had been.

France believed that the Sykes-Picot *"treaty"* had been severely riddled after the war, and she was trying to use that tool as a basis for negotiation over what was left of the spoils.

The French Government felt she had lost much of what she wanted and entitled. Despite the British attitude, by August 1919, France was still expecting to get a Syrian coast strip from just north of Akka to Latakia. Perhaps, the entire problem was the inability of the two 'contestants' – England and France – to distinguish between their needs and their greed, and they both showed callous desire that they hoped might grow pious very fast with time.

Despite Sykes-Picot, political tension was brewing between the French and the British. London believed that a French rule over Syria would not be acceptable by the people. Undeniably, some members of the group of officials whom France sent out in 1919 to Beirut had been blunderers to the French authorities' detriment. Unexpectedly, the group of French officials had intensified the native opposition to France. Their vigorous propaganda measures had been indiscreet and shortsighted. Charges of the continuance of the potency of *"baksheesh"* (bribery or pay-off, or grease ones' palm) were current.

Both the French and the Syrians knew that the British were engaged in anti-French propaganda. Unquestionably, the British officers disapproved of Syria's French occupation and did not desire its occurrence. The Syrians relied upon British statesmanship in Paris to see the French leaving, perhaps to Cilicia over in Asia Minor.

At a 1920 conference in San Remo - Italy, mandates were assigned.

France was taking the northern part of Syria, and Britain was taking Palestine and Iraq.

Approved by the League of Nations, the mandates were described as class "A," meaning that France and Britain would eventually relinquish control and grant full independence.

The Wilsonian plan of self-determination was largely ignored. The Americans were not even represented at the conference. The US delegate bided time in a hotel garden awaiting instruction from Washington while the Mideast's most critical issues were settled.

Meanwhile, the Arabs refused to give up the idea of immediate independence.

On March 7, 1920, a General Syria Congress, meeting in Damascus, - Speaker Hashem al-Attasi - proclaimed Feisal King of the Arab Kingdom of Syria, including Palestine. The declaration came at least five years late.

It came too late, but it came while Syria remained defiant. Had it been declared in 1915 during the British troops' advance toward Mesopotamia, the Levant's history would have differed. At that time - (1915) - France had been weak and searched for a European identity.

Now – (1920) - considering the proclamation as a direct threat to her rights in Syria, France overwhelmed the Arab Army and entered Damascus to depose the King.

Hypocrisy is not a religion, but here is a dispatch from Paris to the Syrian-Lebanese League of North America signed by three influential leaders in the Syrian movement and made public in New York on March 23, 1920:

> Committee of Greater Lebanon telegraphs that by an act of violence, Feisal convened the self-appointed assembly, which proclaimed him King of Syria. The committee asks France to protect their rights, announcing its determination to repulse the encroachment of arms. Sanguinary troubles between Christians and Muslims are expected. A later telegram says the Nuseirieh *(sic)* section *(Alawites)* and the Druses *(sic)* of Houran and Lebanon have joined the Christians' proclamation. The persecution of Christians in the Hedjaz (Hijaz) occupation zone surpasses the Turkish regime. Beirut complains that American missionary activities are encouraging Feisal to the detriment of Christian interests.[37]

---

[37] The American Archives… The Baltimore Sun – Maryland, March 24, 1920.

The dispatch was signed by Emir Tawfik Arslan, who was delegated "by the Druses *(sic)* of Lebanon to represent them in Paris, during the settlement of the Turkish question. Chikri Genam *(sic)* – *Shukri Ghanem*, who was head of the Syrian peace delegation in Paris, and Dr. E. G. Tabet, former president of the Syrian-Lebanese League of North America."[38]

> The Syrian-Lebanese League of North America program provides for the establishment in Syria of autonomous governments – Mount Lebanon, with its ancient boundaries (greater Lebanon), Damascus, Aleppo, etc., under the guidance and protection of France. And the "independence of the Syrian question from the Hedjaz movement, under the formula of pan-Arabian, Arabic-speaking peoples, or otherwise."[39]

In September 1920, news traveling from London to Beirut mentioned that a letter from the Prime Minister of France, Alexandre Millerand, to the Maronite Archbishop of Arka[40] had been made public. Millerand said that France desires the extension of Lebanon into a Greater Lebanon, which would include Jebel Akkar in the north and Mount Hermon in the south, and the town of Tripoli in the north. France was keen on getting done with Lebanon by giving the impression she wanted to do it without creating any waves as she progressed. But that was not the case. Only six months before Millerand's letter, France mentioned that there had been sanguinary speculations about

---

[38] -Ibid-

[39] *Associated Press* – Ref Springfield Missouri Republican, Wednesday, March 24, 1920.

[40] Arka is at North Lebanon and is one of the ancient places that go back to the Roman times. Roman Emperor Alexandre Severus (Reign 222 to 235) was born there, and during the Crusades, he used Tell Arka as strategically significant castle.

possible troubles between Christian and Muslims in Syria because of the boycott declared against France and England by Feisal, then newly elected King of Syria. Millerand's letter, being untimely published, intended to show that the Christians were in a precarious situation and would, therefore, need France's protection.

The record of France as an occupation force in Syria has not been kind.

Her policy has been "divide and rule." France began by dividing Syria into three or four states, roughly corresponding to the Syrian people's religious affiliations. This division had nothing to do with the military Roadmaps of the *now*-defunct Sykes-Picot.

Again, hypocrisy is not a religion; by reiterating propaganda works – parrot fashion - without even counting the cost, many Lebanese were inclined to believe anything the French had said.

Thus, Secular France turned to mold her mandate territory along religious lines.

Thus, Lebanon's former autonomous Ottoman vilayet was enlarged – by the addition of Beirut and other ports and multiple inland districts toward the east and south-east, into the State of Greater Lebanon.

Maronite Christians dominated greater Lebanon – a lot of them longtime French allies – but also took in many Muslims for economic and strategic reasons. The new configuration won approval from the Maronites but disfavored from many Arab and Syrian nationalists, Muslims, and Christians, who felt cut off from Damascus. Arab nationalists on both sides of the line also believed that someone had truncated their natural state. For a time, the French also split present-day Syria into *countries*.[41]

One year before, the King-Crane Commission produced their seventy-page Report of August 28, 1919, in which

---

[41] Aleppo and Damascus, for example, were separate but dependent 'states' from 1920 to 1925.

the American section of Inter-allied Commission of "mandates in Turkey" laid out the views of two Americans[42] on the Syrian portion of their task; they wrote:

> The American Section of the International Commission on Mandates in Turkey, so that their mission may be clearly understood, is furnishing to the press the following statement, which is intended to define as accurately as possible the nature of their task, as given to them by President Wilson.

> The American people - having no political ambitions in Europe or the Near East, preferring, if that were possible, to keep clear of all European, Asian, or African entanglements. But sincerely desiring that the most permanent peace and the largest results for humanity shall come out of this war *(WWI)* - recognize that they cannot altogether avoid responsibility for just settlements among the nations following the war and under the League of Nations. In that spirit, they approach the problems of the Near East.

The intention was to refute 'allegations' that were widespread in Europe.
Recent dispatches from Paris indicated that the investigation of some American mandates in the Near East was being brought to completion by the American Peace Commission. The subject of a Mandate would soon come before the American people for consideration decision.

---

[42] The two Americans are - Dr. Henry Chutchill King and Charles Crane. During 1918-1919 King was director of religious work for YMCA in France, and Crane was a member of the American Section of the Peace Conference, American Ambassador to China (1920-1921).

Newspapers' correspondents in close touch with members of the American delegates were spreading the news that the report of the special American Commission sent to Turkey to study the question of a Mandate was

"for an American Mandate over the entire Turkish Empire, which is *supposed* to be under a British mandate. Mr. Crane, who headed this commission, said: We found the opinion of the best Turks themselves for an American mandate as the wisest solution to their troubles. Although, of course, there is a dominant sentiment among the Turks, the extent of which cannot be accurately gauged, for the continuance of their independence."

An International Commission was projected by the Council of Four of the Peace Conference to study conditions in the Turkish Empire regarding possible mandates. The American Section of that Commission is in the Near East simply, and solely, to get accurate and definite information concerning the conditions, relations, and desires *of all the peoples and classes concerned* so that President Wilson and the American people may act with full knowledge of the facts in any policy they may be called upon hereafter to adopt concerning the problems of the Near East whether in the Peace Conference or the later League of Nations.

This statement of the mission of the Commission is in complete harmony with the following paragraph from the Covenant of the League of Nations, mainly referring to portions of the former Turkish Empire:

"Certain communities formerly belonging to the Turkish Empire have reached a stage of development where their existence as independent nations can be provisionally recognized subject to the rendering of administrative advice and assistance by *a Mandatory* until they can stand alone. The wishes of these communities must be a principal consideration in the *selection* of the Mandatory."

Therefore, the Americans sought *the Mideast people's voice* on any decisions on post-war settlements in the region.
Among the Turkish Empire's subject peoples, the desire was almost unanimous for the Americans to become *administrators.*
But, in some areas of Palestine, the first choice was for England as Mandatory power, and in specific Catholic regions like Lebanon, the first choice "is for France; but for the far greater part of the whole empire, the first option is for America."

On Lebanon:

3. The Lebanon Programs: There are three distinct types of Lebanese programs that appear in the petitions:

(a) The French Independent Greater Lebanon. This program asks for *complete* independence and *separation* from Syria for the Greater Lebanon, including the Valley of Bekaa *(Beqaa)* and in some instances, Tripoli. *France is requested* as the Mandatory Power. 139 of the 146 petitions received in O. E. T. A.[43] West contain this

---

[43] O.E.T.A. "The area and towns covered by the Commission's inquiry are shown in the itinerary for June 10 to July 21, 1919, and in the table of the towns, classified according to the different divisions of the Occupied Enemy Territory Administrations-British, French, and Arab These tables show that the Commission visited 36 of the more important towns of Syria, scattered through all the military areas, and

program, with practically identical wording. Of these twenty, are three varieties of printed forms.

(b) The Independent Lebanon Program. Another distinct program asks for the same points *except* for a French Mandate. 33 of the 36 petitions with the wording of this program are two varieties of printed forms. In eight instances, requests for a mandate are added in writing.

(c) The Autonomous Lebanon Program. This program asks for a greater Lebanon as an *autonomous province within* a united Syrian State. No mandate is mentioned. Forty-nine petitions are copies of this program, three of them on a printed form.

Hence, France behaved adroitly with the King-Crane Report, one year after its publication ignoring the Sykes-Picot dotted lines.

Blaming the Sykes-Picot Roadmaps has been an accusation reiterated throughout the Levant. It is found in the mouth of every person who supports the opposite opinion to the King-Crane Commission on Lebanon.
France's real action concerning *Greater Lebanon* had nothing to do with the colored zones and the dotted lines of the roadmaps called Sykes-Picot. Initially, the American Commission had acted independently thereof.

---

heard delegations from other important centers. It should be noted that the list does not include at all the names of hosts of villages in the vicinity of towns visited, which were also represented by delegations before the Commission. Our records show that there were 1,520 such villages. Cilicia was briefly included in the Syrian inquiry, because it is disputed territory claimed both by Syria and by the Turkish-speaking portion of the former Turkish Empire" Ref. The King-Crane Commission Report, August 28, 1919

By October 1924, the international press spoke of Greater Lebanon as "the former Syria section." The media were impressed by how Beirut and the Lebanon Hills – as were then described – wanted a national anthem and was willing to pay for it.

Although a French-mandated territory of about 4,000 square miles, with a high commissioner sent from France administering her, "Le Gouverneur du Grand Liban" found that the "Marseillaise" did not do or was not enough. He had encouraged a local firm of music publishers to announce a prize contest for the best "national hymn." Two thousand Syrian francs were offered for the best song.

The composition of Lebanon politics was like European Duchies without a crown. In the distribution of privileges, everyone, Shia, Sunni, Maronite, Orthodox, there was one primary factor: Sovereign and his consorts are concerned - each *Zaeem* (Boss) regarded the Duchy as private property. The 'bosses' were well entrenched and could dig their fingers into many political pies, and each voice could limit the direction and tie up future Parliament. A seat in Parliament or a public office was the big fish and Beirut's upstart new oligarchy's mastermind.

Here must be noted that the Sykes-Picot roadmaps could not have possibly created what had already been entrenched like the marrow in a human bone.

The mosaic political structure of Greater Lebanon was a byproduct of the multiple cultures and tenets that existed within the Ottoman Empire, and which the Turks, over centuries of harsh oppression, had failed to retain.

Chapter 10. *Render to Caesar the things that are Caesar's*

Students at Oxford and other European Universities, or Al-Azhar,[44] whether of Levantine or rural Arab origin, in the early 1920s, could not refute what their fellow-Indian-undergraduates had been mentioning. Indian students spoke about the suggested distinction, in India, between Hindu and Muslims, as primarily a British invention, imported for an imperial policy of *divide and rule*.

France has also been considered likewise.

Anything the elite could fathom might not have been possibly filtered down to the grassroots – the ordinary citizens.

When her troops were making conquests in Asia, England had some excuse during the war, but the reason did not hold in the post-war period.

France could not fathom why the British continued to occupy and control territory, which should have passed under French administration? The French asked why the British had spent money lavishly for propaganda on the native populations whom the French should administer?

The answer is because the Muslims of Arabia rejected the French Bourbon and accepted the British Anglo-Saxons.

There was one significant point in British propaganda. Britain encouraged *the Syrians to think* they were competent for complete *self-government* and started a movement for that liberty. In the Syrians' mind, they wanted to teach that Great Britain, contrary to the French

---

[44] "Al-Azhar University is a university in Cairo, Egypt. Associated with Al-Azhar Mosque in Islamic Cairo, it is Egypt's oldest degree-granting university and is renowned as "Sunni Islam's most prestigious university""

aspirations, had never preplanned Syria's occupation properly.

The French asked themselves, what would be the result of Great Britain occupying Syria? England, in the French eyes, knew very well that *self-government* would be a failure. Why? As was perceived by France and Great Britain, if the Turks, Jews, and Christians were left to themselves, they would soon have a turmoil of disorder demanding troops' intervention to save life and property. If the British knew that, then why encourage *self-government*?

British forces in Mesopotamia, being the nearest neighbors, would be the ones to do the intervening, which would be an excuse for permanent British occupation and administration. Such mishmash has never had anything to do with Sykes-Picot, which addressed the military rather than political issues.

Besides, there had been hiatus where self-government – by *inexperienced* Syrians and Mesopotamians - were tried and failed, a fact against considering Sykes-Picot as a *"treaty"* with France.

The French firmly believed that the British had intentionally and untimely encouraged *inexperienced* people to govern themselves so that Britain could sooner than later put her firm hand on such governments under the pretext of civil disturbances in the disputed areas. And that was much worse than the legend of *"Divide-and-rule."*

On the military scene, Great Britain was much stronger than the French. Thanks to India, and the British dominions, England was certainly capable in case of extreme need of raising 3,000,000 men more, something the French and even the Teutonic empires and their allies had no such reserves of strength, physical or financial as the war had shown.

But in India, the story was different.

India was a member of the British throne as a military nation of approved capabilities. England and the dominions had already put 3,000,000 men under arms, something that France could not match.

The whole records entitled the French to assume that the same English prevarications they saw in Egypt would still prevail. France regarded that the British cardinal policy was to protect India.

England, in the present Asia Minor situation, saw an opportunity to put a finishing touch on her work of the last thirty years to keep Russia from penetrating India. England knew Russia (post-revolution) was not out of existence permanently and feared her coming back to average power and a resumption of her old Asiatic aims. France, also knowing Russia would come back sooner or later, was not for a Turkish policy, which would leave nothing for Russia in the future. Russia's population was almost inexhaustible.

Like new Russia, France excluded all sectarian teaching, the ingraining of all those forms of religious opinion that separated the country's religious denominations from each other. They also banned all formal religious and theological teaching. All books taught any way of theological views or ideas, removed but kept strictly neutral ground on religion and theology.

In this respect, France met resistance in the Arab world.

Conversely, England confirmed her status as the angel guardian of the Muslim world.

Excluding Greater Lebanon, France still focused on Sykes-Picot as a *"treaty,"* – and not as military roadmaps of temporary nature. The French regarded the British's first violation was to recognize the independence of the (Muslim) Kingdom of the Hijaz, which included much of the French zone. They even recognized Damascus, which was French territory, as an Arabian capital. The French mentioned they had submitted because of war, and European conditions, in general, made France helpless to do otherwise.

Before the War, the Levant, now described as Syria and the Lebanon, Trans-Jordan, and Palestine, comprised roughly the *Vilayets* of Beirut and Damascus and the independent *Sanjak* of Jerusalem. In these Provinces, as integral parts of the Turkish Empire, no proper formalities were required by persons leaving one Province for another.

The Middle East's post-war settlement[45] created new boundaries between Palestine and Syria and Lebanon, and similarly between Palestine and Trans-Jordan. Therefore, persons crossing from one *country* to another were now passing from their "home" countries to "foreign" countries. Thus, new office-holding oligarchies were formed alongside the new 'borders.'

The new boundaries, however, were not those shown by the dotted lines in the Sykes-Picot roadmaps. Instead, they were agreed upon at Versailles considering a combination of factors from the King-Crane Report and the latest colored Zones shown on the latest roadmaps drawn by Sykes-Picot. Those colored dotted-lines accounted for clannishness, family affiliations, feudalism, confessional denominations, various allegiances, and other practical exigencies.

By 1925, since the establishment of the entity of Greater Lebanon in September 1920, there had been differences among the elite of all confessions about her identity. Is the burgeoning country of fewer than one million inhabitants an Arab? Is she pertinent to the Arab world? But first, is there an Arab World at all? What would her system of governance be? If an Arab, would she be a Kingdom? Or Parliamentarian! Or Confessional! Or a combination of both? Would the President be elected by the people or through their representatives?

---

[45] Here, the Term: The *Middle East* includes present days' Iraq, Syria, Israel, Palestine, Iran, Turkey, and Egypt.

At the French and American universities in Beirut, the educated elite students learned that Oligarchy in Germany stood in the road, and the future of world peace remained in doubt. In combination with a similar handful in Austria-Hungary, that selfsame Oligarchy had been capable of starting the war.

How about 'Democracy?'

At the French and American universities, the educated elite students learned a good deal about liberty, freedom, and democracy. Nevertheless, very often, their talk has been of the flag-waving kind, and they could not translate their conversations into deeds, other than cries for Arab (or Syrian) Nationalism.

Just what did they mean by Democracy and Nationalism? Was it the right thing to do as they please, regardless of the rights of others? The educated elite noticed that France herself, who preach democracy and nationalism, most noisily failed to practice it or even understand it in times of war.

Then something else surfaced. In Lebanon and Syria, the factor of foreign subordination remained unresolved. France and England feared that doctrinal and ideological denominations that could solicit external financing would make the outside giver able to run the country, *"qui donne ordonne."* This qualm applies in the Levant, where the legend 'business-manship' applies to a population of the mercantile atmosphere.

The French government also feared that such a small state like greater Lebanon might cause friction between the super-powers that had just squared their differences, so to speak, at Versailles. Overtly, greater Lebanon to France and the Maronite church, after the war, was in a relationship like "render to Caesar the things that are Caesar's, and to God the things that are God's."

Covertly, to the mosaic Lebanese society, France became both Caesar and God in the absence of one, underlying, structured administration within greater Lebanon.

Chapter 11. *Lebanon and Syria – Post 1920.*

The situation in Syria was disturbing.

It will be remembered that the Syrians had rejected the idea of the Mandatory government and demanded national independence. It was only after some fighting that the French were able in 1920 to occupy Damascus and compel King Feisal to leave the country.

The circumstances were these: any political's pronouncement must deal with a matter of faith or morals. Not political or social beliefs or anything close to that kind, and the Church or the Mosque must clarify that it is speaking to the whole – that is, the chair of St. Peter in Rome or the Mufti of Mecca. It was case-sensitive, notably after the demise of the Caliphate when a lot of Muslims felt betrayed.

The Mandatory French administration was organized by territorial division, under which four "states" were ultimately constituted — a vast inland "Syria." Two little sea-board "states," Lebanon (where the tradition of French friendship was oldest and most vital) and an Alawite "state" north of Lebanon, and a separate enclave in the hill-country for the Druze.

In each of these units, elected Representative Councils had been established by 1925; the administration was in the hands of Arab ministers. The powers of the French officials were nominally limited to supervision and advice.

By 1925, there were indications that the French in Syria were surmounting a rebellion crisis.

This mastering over a crisis happened while the controversy between Turkey and Iraq over the boundaries in the Mosul district, in which Great Britain was concerned, entered its critical stage sometime in

November 1925. And when this matter was taken up at Geneva by the Council of the League of Nations. Sunni-Shia relations were not raw. It reverberated within the French and the British minds, as demonstrated in the Young Baghdadi party in Syria, which did not include a single Shia amongst its members. *"The Shia of Mesopotamia, who number 1¾ million, will accept no form of Arab Government based on Sunni denomination."* *"Many years will now elapse before the people of this country [Iraq] will be at least as well equipped as the people of Egypt and India now are for Western forms of Government. But for the present, the population is so deeply divided by racial and religious cleavages. The Shia majority, after 200 years of Sunni domination [Ottoman Empire], are so little accustomed to hold a high office that any attempt to introduce institutions on the lines desired by the advanced Sunni politicians of Syria would involve the concentration of power in the hands of a few persons whose ambitions and methods could rapidly bring about the collapse of organized Government."*[46]

In Syria, however, Henri de Jouvenel, the new French High Commissioner, who had replaced General Maurice Sarrail, has had the broad view of realizing the essential unity of the two Allied Mandatory Powers in the ex-Arab provinces of the Ottoman Empire.

He did not go to Beirut until he had visited London, Cairo, and Jerusalem. Since arriving in Syria, he had lost no time in opening a door for reconciliation between the British and French views on Syria and Lebanon.

His work had been made as difficult as previous French High Commissioners' policy at Beirut, instructed or indulged by previous Governments in Paris, who have had a rough experience in Iraq, between Muslims.

---

[46] The British Archives [excerpts] CAB/24/96, Image Ref 0004 of November 15, 1919 notes from G.L. Bell entitled "Syria 1919."

But why the policy of the previous French High Commissioners had not been accepted?

The reason is this: While this geographic allocation was calculated to win the Lebanese Catholics to the French cause and drive in a wedge between them and their Druze and Muslim [Sunni and Shia] fellow-country-men, there was a severe curtailment of self-government.

The self-government refers to the one smaller Lebanon had enjoyed under the previous dispensation, when Turkish suzerainty was nominal, while the Great Powers of Europe guaranteed the Constitution.

Thus, even for the Lebanese Christians, the establishment of the French Mandate was a mixed blessing, while for the Muslims and the Druze, it was decidedly less desirable than

the Ottoman *regime.*

Under the Ottoman *regime,* the Druze of the Jabal Houran, in the extreme south-east of Syria, toward the desert, had maintained, by their military prowess, a *de facto* autonomy. Such autonomy as complete as that which had been secured to Lebanon by international treaties, and it was here that the present trouble began – owing, it seems, to the shortcomings of a French officer who was deputed to control the Houran, and to the roughness of General Sarrail when the Druze complained.

For instance, practically, a significant proportion of Arab immigrants into Palestine came from the Houran.

These people went in considerable numbers to Haifa, where they worked in the port. It was, however, necessary to realize that the extent of the yearly exodus from the Houran depended mainly on the state of the crops there. *"In a good year, the amount of illegal immigration into Palestine is negligible and confined to the younger members of large families whose presence is not required in the fields. Most persons in this category would remain permanently in Palestine, wages there being considerably higher than in Syria. According to a reliable estimate, as many as ten or eleven thousand Hourani may go to*

Palestine temporarily in search of work in a bad year.
The Deputy Inspector-General of the Criminal
Investigation Department has recently estimated that the
number of Hourani illegally in the country now is roughly
2,500. "[47]

There was no overpowering motive to conceal men's
identity from Houran going to Palestine unless they were
compelled. The distinction was less than semantic.

In Lebanon, it was different.

Throughout the ensuing rebellion, the Druze, not the
Muslims, have taken the lead, and their attacks have been
directed toward the new territories, containing a
considerable Druze and Muslim population. Druze
sentiments went toward Great Britain. Unable to protect
these territories with their regular troops, before de
Jouvenel's arrival, the French authorities had taken the
disastrous step of serving out arms to the local Christians,
thus virtually abandoning control of the situation,
allowing it to drift, by proxy.

At best, toward unrestrained brigandage, and, at worst,
into a religious war.

On December 3, 1925, de Jouvenel began by meeting the
Elective Council of the Greater Lebanon and empowering
it to act virtually as a constituent assembly, to await its
recommendations before formulating any detailed
program of his own.

The 1925 Lebanon was to receive back at least as full
autonomy as it enjoyed before the war. And while France
would still control its foreign relations, the French
officials who were to assist in its internal administration
were to have only advisory and not executive powers.

In other words, Lebanon [with a French accent] was to
obtain a status like that which Iraq has enjoyed under the
British Mandate, since the bureaucratic government on
the Anglo-Indian model, introduced during the war, was

---

[47] Courtesy of the British Archives CAB/24/270, June 1937.

replaced by the present treaty between the Governments of London and Baghdad.

Having opened this prospect to Lebanon, which has not revolted, de Jouvenel had intimated that the terms no less favorable will be accorded to the Syrian patriots – not brigands – now in revolt and with a French accent.

The several Syrian States should then be left free to form a federation. France should agree to support the application by Federated Syria to become a member of the League of Nations, not later than a similar request on Iraq's part was supported by Great Britain. Egypt's British administration's success stories appealed to the French who wished to copy/paste it in Lebanon and Syria, but with a French accent.

Still, the security situation in Lebanon was different from Syria. The Maronites had no alternative but to establish a state-based on evolution, not revolution.

Naturally, after the famine, the war ills, and the Turks' oppression, the people of greater Lebanon were not in a radical position. The combination of a country was one that deserved the attention and protection of an international forum because a Greater Lebanon meant coexistence between the Christians and the Muslims that the Ottoman Empire, principally by a lot of her Muslim *fanatic* clerics, did not fully succeed to accomplish, at least over the last century.

The fate of Greater Lebanon was left to the French to manage. And the French, friends with the Maronites, decided that the Maronites would be able to stand defiant to King Feisal, who had always been reticent to entrust France.

Thus, France, who has been secular in appearance all over, preferred to mask herself and establish *a quasi-state* in Greater Lebanon based on confessionals.

The main reason was the volte-face of French business entrepreneurs for private trade with the Orient and a protection wall against all the rest of the world, something they couldn't do in Egypt.

In Lebanon, secular France was something else – and she represented a volte-face diplomacy' attitude to temporary issues.

France cared for Maronite identification at a time a lot of Maronite scholars were Arab nationalists. And she attempted to curry favor with the Muslim Sunni as if they were Maronite scholars.

Moreover, when French philanthropy did come into the Church, they tended to secularize it. And that would continue until French schools and universities would organically assimilate the Muslims, and convert the Christians into French flesh and blood and reclaim them as France's children in all respects – notably in the army.

France has never had an army adequate to the defense of her possessions.

After Napoleon's blunders, she never was a dangerous militaristic nation based on her Nationals' workforce alone, and never could be in a post-1914 world war. Her people were tired and depleted but not defeated. Probably the chief reason why Clemenceau's cabinet had executed such *volte-face* – from confessional to secular power - in Greater Lebanon had been the impossibility of getting troops, conscripted or otherwise – for service in the Levant. Or, indeed, for use anywhere unless when the French possessions were directly threatened.

In Greater Lebanon, France considered the Maronites as her political tool - her outsourcing in the Levant - as were the military roadmaps of Sykes-Picot had been her legislative instrument in the Mideast.

Right or wrong, the Maronites saw that a strong France would oppress them less than a divisive and turbulent Sultan.

Chapter 12. *Wilson's Fourteen Points*

Now, let's go a short time back – 1918.

By October 25, 1918, the Hohenzollerns' power was broken; Prussian militarism's menace was lifted. If the Allies have had the courage and wisdom to lay hold on this occasion, Europe's peace would be guaranteed for future generations.

The world could start afresh with President Woodrow Wilson's fourteen points [January 8, 1918] as its Magna Charta.[48]

Wilson, still in poor health conditions, had to grapple with an uncertain political situation in Germany. In Berlin, the new government tried to interpret his fourteen points as not implying Alsace-Lorraine or Poland's surrender.

At 3 o'clock on Monday, October 28, 1918, Germany was left to *fight* single-handed against Britain, France, Belgium, Italy, Serbia, Portugal, Greece, and the United Kingdom.

On Wednesday, Berlin learned from President Wilson that, subject to two modifications,[49] the Allies were prepared to *grant* Peace on his terms, and that the armistice conditions might be had from French General Foch. Germany's representatives immediately left for the Western Front, "and if there is any trace of sanity remaining in her rulers, the war must within a few days be over."

---

[48] ANNEX IV.

[49] As reported in the press, the two modifications were democratization of the Austrian Constitution and the various proposed amendments to the Imperial Constitution (German) become law, so that Germany, in name, at least, would become a country governed by representatives' institutions.

Initially, Wilson didn't know that the French and the British's secret talks did not stop with America's entry into the war. The confidential discussions did not stop even after accepting the 'Fourteen Points'[50] as the basis for the Peace, with their open diplomacy provisions regarding Turkey's disposal.

The talks even continued secretly between Great Britain and France after the Peace Conference began.

In a nutshell, France and Great Britain were playing politics behind Wilson's back.

Almost ten months before the armistice, Woodrow Wilson had directly addressed what he perceived to be the World War causes in a speech to Congress.

Wilson called for the abolition of secret treaties, a reduction in armaments, an adjustment in Colonial claims in the interests of native peoples and colonists, and freedom of the seas.

Wilson also made proposals that would ensure world peace in the future.

For example, he proposed removing economic barriers between nations; the promise of "self-determination" for those oppressed minorities; and a world organization that would provide a collective security system for all countries.

Wilson's Fourteen Points were designed to undermine the Central Powers' will to continue the war and inspire the Allies to victory. The Fourteen Points were broadcast throughout the world and, figuratively speaking, were showered with rockets and shells behind the enemy's lines. *delusional*

---

[50] President Woodrow Wilson's Fourteen Points (1918)). In this January 8, 1918, speech on War Aims and Peace Terms, President Wilson set down Fourteen Points as a blueprint for world peace that was to be used for peace negotiations after World War I.

Indeed, Versailles' feedback was confusing; the discussions were as unclear as to the Armenians' quest to do something about establishing a unified "nation" for themselves.

However, the vagueness of the Italians' requests regarding the recovery of Fiume's port, and the city, opened the question concerning the Armenian claims' confusion. It was so because the French had been alarmed by the British intentions and public appetite to acquire more than was necessary. France was fearful that the British would become too powerful in that part of the world – the Levant and Arabia.

Thus, in January 1918, the 'Fourteen Points' were set forth by President Wilson as a proposed basis for peace. And Lloyd George told the world (January 5) that the secret treaties no longer fettered the Allies in discussing Turkey's future.

But, as far as the Levant and Arabia were concerned, these 'secret treaties' kept right on throughout 1919 – the dotted lines and colored zones - were taken from the most recent and advantageous roadmaps (in the plural) for the spoils to be divided.

Thus, the roadmaps that were set to serve military purposes, now, in the absence of the principal player – Mark Sykes – were considered by France to be of political significance. It must be recalled that the roadmaps had addressed military challenges above ground, and the authors, Mark Sykes and George Picot, never thought of the spoils hidden underground.

And the underground spoils were indeed gorgeous.

Dividing the spoils was all lies and deceit.

It was one-sided, with one of the partners - Georges Picot – still living and the other - Mark Sykes – dead.

It was also an opportunity of greed - a matter of taking vengeance and levying unreasonable war reparation costs upon Germany and her people.

It was all like an assassin who takes life easily.

England and France only lied to King Feisal and the Arabs, the Armenians, the Jews, the Americans, and the Italians. The promises of the French and English governments were indecently loaded with dynamite.

Indeed, they had bound themselves to accept America's 'Fourteen Points.'

But, also, they had solemnly bound themselves to repudiate secret dealings and abide by the provisions of Turkey, which the American President – Woodrow Wilson, had laid down in Point XII.[51]

After they had made that contract – after Wilson had arrived in Paris on December 13, 1918,[52] they were accused of breaking their pledges, concluding new arrangements behind Wilson's back, and double-crossing him with cheerful cynicism.

Therefore, from the high days on which the curtain rang down upon the vast grim drama of the war – November 11, 1918, until it went to the tragedy of the Peace Conference at Versailles – Paris on January 12, 1919 - two full months had elapsed. President Wilson had arrived in Europe on December 13, 1918, ready and expected to begin the conference at once, or within a few days – and a month slipped away.

Moreover, the allied diplomats were well satisfied to wait until they had secured the last grain of advantage under the most extreme armistice terms known in modern war.

---

[51] Point 12 called for Turkey to remain sovereign, but other peoples throughout the Middle East, long under the Ottoman yolk, should also be allowed to develop autonomously. Wilson also demanded that the Dardanelles, the straits that connect the Black Sea with the Aegean Sea, should be open to navigation by all nations.

[52] The vast grim drama of the war ended on November 11, 1918.

While President Wilson had indeed laid down the peace principles, the military men, who were then effectively in control, had made the terms of the truce.

And the Armistice was in effect a preliminarily imposed treaty in which not only the usual and immediate military and naval terms were prescribed, but in broad outline, many of the boundaries were subsequently demanded, and even financial and economic provisions were added. President Wilson was thus partly defeated by the military men - or at least by many politicians in military clothing *(Clemenceau)*; his task had been made more difficult before arriving in Europe.

Moreover, Turkey's breakup meant a new arrangement in Egypt and some new possibilities of opening to communication and exploitation of another old empire – that of Persia. Wilson knew that the Mediterranean Sea control also turned upon possession of Asia Minor, Syria, and Palestine.

At that time, many people wondered why the United States Senate rejected the Treaty of Versailles!

Like Wilson, a significant portion of the American population knew that Germany had had a clear vision of the Near East's enormous importance. Before the war, she had projected and partly built the Berlin-Baghdad railroad and had attempted "peaceful penetration" by every means in her power.

The Great War had even been described as "primarily a struggle for the domination of the Near East."

But Sykes-Picot did not deal with the political allocation of territory in a *dotted line* fashion. It did not imply *'some agreement'*[53] on the French and British parts to allow

---

[53] See ANNEX III.

other nations any rights in all this significant part of the old (former) Turkish (Ottoman) Empire.

The authors of the roadmaps were not qualified to do such massive work. Indeed, their dotted lines were intended to keep pace with the variations in the field of operation and changed on the spur of the moment.

Such *'some agreement'* undoubtedly meant their ally – Italy.

Hence plans were made to begin economic development by building a new railroad from Baghdad direct to Aleppo. Great Britain could get a connection out to the sea at Alexandretta for her Mesopotamian oil. The Italians would also benefit.

To get this done, Lloyd George offered Smyrna and mainly another Turkish territory to the Italians. Balfour, his Foreign Minister, it will be remembered, was just then in America, helping to cheer along with American participation in the war. He told President Wilson and Clemenceau, during a meeting of the Council of May 11, 1919 (Secret Minutes):

> While I was away, Mr. Lloyd George, no doubt
> for reasons which appeared to him sufficient, had,
> at St. Jean Maurienne, agreed to let the Italians
> have Smyrna under certain conditions.

But even this did not satisfy the Italians.

The negotiations dragged along. Finally, a secret agreement was reached, giving Italy not only Smyrna but also a zone influence of high-value north of it, inhabited chiefly by Greeks and Turks.

This agreement was, however, to be dependent upon the approval of the Russians.

But the Russian Government, which had just been overthrown by the revolutionists, never gave that consent. The result was that a considerable controversy developed at the Peace Conference about whether or not the promises of the Italians at St. Jean de Maurienne were binding upon France and Great Britain.

During the weeks of delay in December and January, the French were making good the physical possession of the Alsace-Lorraine, the Sarre coalfields, Dalmatia, and the Rhine frontier.

Germany surrendered on November 11, 1918.
The 'surrender' was in the form of an armistice between the Allies and Germany – also known as the Armistice of Compiegne after the location in which it was signed – and the agreement ended the fighting on the Western Front. However, Germany surrendered under the express condition that she had to be guaranteed by Woodrow Wilson's Fourteen Points of January 8, 1918.
The war ended on November 11, 1918.
With the American army in Sedan, the British in possession of the forts of Maubeuge, and Belgium rapidly cleared "of the Hun invaders," it didn't make any difference whether Germany accepts the armistice term of Foch as far as a result is concerned.
Germany was whipped. Foch had won a complete and absolute military victory. The German army's power was crushed.
"This will end," said the hard-headed late James Hill,[54] a long time ago, "when somebody gets licked," and, exactly, that is what had happened.

But the submission of Austria was different.
Austria had explicitly refused surrender under the Fourteen Points.

---

[54] James Hill was a Canadian-American, the CEO of 'Great Northern Railway.' Because of the large magnitude of his business and the financial control exerted by the Hill lines, Hill became known during his lifetime as "The Empire Builder." (1838-1916).

She had officially yielded about one week before the Germans did. Austria surrendered to Italy, not the Allies, unconditionally.

The surrender took the form of an Armistice of, best known as 'The Armistice of Villa Giusti,' which ended warfare between Italy and Austria-Hungary on the Italian Front.

It was signed on 3 November 1918, outside of Padua in the Veneto, northern Italy, and took effect 24 hours later.

It was Wilson who, with classic phrase, backed by the authority of recent reelection as the mouthpiece of America, lifted the struggle on to a higher plane, and defined in terms that appealed to the conscience of the world the peace for which America and the Allies were fighting.

And when the war drew to a close, the hopes of humanity were concentrated on the achievement of a "Wilson Peace."

Nevertheless, in his Fourteen Points, Woodrow Wilson did not mention anything about Jerusalem or Palestine. But two English gentlemen of the Jewish faith said, "Sir Herbert Samuel and Lord Reading [Rufus Daniel Isaacs] are Englishmen and Jews. Now, if Jew-ism is a nationality, what about their English-ism? One -ism must be sacrificed for the other, but which for which?

Besides, this promise was made long before British troops came into possession of Palestine. Since this victory was an Allied one, France, Italy, and the Arabs having taken active parts in it, the consent of all should be secured before any *gift* is made. But the Arabs have not been consulted and never will consent, and Russia, *when it wakes up*, will have a word to say."[55]

---

[55] The British Archives (Excerpt) CAB/24/126, Image Ref 0023 Report of the Cairo Conference July 11, 1921.

Chapter 13. *"Acetone converted me to Zionism."*

Another challenge that Sykes and Picot could not have possibly foreseen: The future of the Jews in the Middle East and the distinction between Judaism as a faith and Zionism as a national movement and ideological dogma. World War One almost killed the Zionist movement. Britain had counted on Turkey to come into the war on the side of the Allies.

Instead, the Ottoman Empire sided with the Germans, portending calamity for both the Jews and the British.

To Britain, it meant that her Suez Canal lifeline was in danger.

To the Palestinian Jews, it spelled real disaster.

Every Jew suspected of sympathy with the Allies – the knowledge of little English was considered proof of compassion – was hanged. 12,000 Jews were deported because they were not Turkish citizens, and Zionism itself was declared illegal.

Zionism was born out of the union of two extremes in the nineteenth century Jewry. It was the culmination of ideas as the alienated cosmopolitan intellectuals from Russia and Europe who had nowhere to go, and the toil of the poor Ghetto dwellers who had nothing to lose.

The Ghetto inhabitants were all those in the modern cities and capitals in Russia and Europe.

The Zionists' literature of the late nineteenth and early twentieth century mentions that they purchased Palestine's lands.[56]

---

[56] "…unlike the Russians who exterminated the native Finno-Ugric population in their path as they appropriated the land from Kiev to Moscow, and unlike the Americans who slaughtered the native Indians in their path as they seized the land from the Atlantic to the Pacific, the Jews purchased the land in the path of their colonization drive from

The money to buy Palestinian land came from the Jewish National Fund, an organization founded in 1901 on a suggestion by Theodore Herzl to redeem Israel's land by peoples' subscription to enable workers without the capital to settle there.

Thus, pennies from the poor and gold from the rich poured into the fund. During World War One, the now famed Balfour Declaration was born.

But the Declaration was more than that.

It was an expression of gratitude from the British government to the Jewish people for their part in the Great War.

The story began when England's brilliant chemist – Dr. Chaim Weizmann – had been called into the British War Office to find a way of producing synthetic cordite, an explosive essential to the British war effort, previously manufactured from acetone, a chemical imported from Germany before the war. German submarines were sinking boats carrying Chilean nitrates to England, its only source of explosives. Weizmann discovered such a chemical combination and turned the process over to the British government. Through his Admiralty position, Weizmann met the British ministry's highest personages and succeeded in engaging many members in Zionist aspirations.

"Acetone converted me to Zionism," Lloyd George, Prime Minister of England, was fond of stating dramatically.

One day, the subject of Zionism came up at an informal gathering. Lord Balfour suggested that instead of Palestine, Uganda be used as a place for Jews to settle.

Lebanon to Egypt *and killed none*. The Russians and Americans were successful in solving their problems by impersonal extirpation, but the Jews were not equally successful with their method of just compensation." Reference: The Indestructible Jew by Max I. Dimont, 1971 – New American Library.

"If I were to offer you Paris instead of London, would you take it?' asked Weizmann, to which Balfour, surprised, answered, "But Dr. Weizmann, we have London."

"That's true," replied Weizmann, "but we had Jerusalem when London was a marsh."[57]

In 1917, Weizmann - an ardent Zionist and an eloquent speaker, and a man of high personal magnetism - approached the British government to assume jurisdiction for a National Jewish Home in Palestine. He received a favorable reply.

Through Lord Balfour, the British Foreign Secretary, the British Government let it be known (November 2, 1917) that "His Majesty's Government view with favor the establishment in Palestine of a national home for the Jewish people." Jubilation among the Jews was great.

After World War One, with a vision, England was drawing blueprints for structuring a postwar world, with herself as Victor.

Like Machiavellian plans, England plunged two crucial diplomatic irons into political fire.

First: the secret correspondence between the King of Hijaz, and the former British High Commissioner in Egypt, Sir Arthur Henry McMahon.

In this correspondence (letters), the British guaranteed the Arabs certain Middle Eastern territories if the Arabs would revolt against the Turks, which they subsequently did under the leadership of Lawrence of Arabia.

Second: The Balfour Declaration, being a one-sentence masterpiece in diplomatic deceit.

---

[57] A primitive region filled with treeless land always wet and periodically inundated; characterized by a growth of grasses, bog plant, swamp-plant, and rushes.

106

This *political* carving up of the Middle East complicated the Palestinian question, but not nearly as much as did the Arabs themselves when they exploded diplomatic bombshell by making the correspondence public.

The Arabs insisted that Palestine was part of the promise, though the McMahon correspondence did not mention Palestine by name.[58]

Each of which promised all things to all men.

The Ottoman Empire was neatly dismembered by England and France – not by Sykes-Picot – but in a series of clinical sessions known as *"peace conferences."*

The Middle East was *subdivided like a pasture land for suburban development* into lots called Syria, Lebanon, Transjordan, Iraq, Saudi Arabia, and tied to Britain and France by a series of treaties anchored in Oil Wells.

And the legend: *"Acetone converted me to Zionism,"* to the Jewish people remained a revival of the flowery praise, and to the Palestinians reverberating roar of the stormy days.

Again, the subdivisions had nothing to do with the *dotted lines and military colored zones* embodied in the *military* roadmaps of Sykes-Picot.

In the eyes of British diplomacy and the Americans' pragmatism, Sykes-Picot, after the war, was the tail that wags the dog.

Wilson had left behind him a neglected field in the Levant. And since the date of the Armistice, America was only a novice in the war. America and the Arabs were still in the high tide of that passion. England and France and Italy and Germany had begun to ebb as early as 1915, and the Arabs became belligerent as soon as the Balfour Declaration.

---

[58] In 1922, Palestine embraces 45,000 square miles which supported 750,000 people.

Thus, five years after the war, the Levant was not a safer and better place.

The roar of the crowds thronging the major Arab capitals' streets was audible from Lord Balfour's hotel, a quarter of a mile from the Damascus square.

On Tuesday, March 31, 1925, Lord Balfour had arrived at the large open theater on the eastern slope of Mount Scopus Hebrew University in Jerusalem and delivered a speech. Few, even among the critics - Jewish and Gentile - of Zionism read without sympathy his words. The creation of a "Jewish State" in Palestine was undoubtedly a highly debatable objective, and the British Government had never committed itself to it, either in the celebrated "Balfour Declaration" of 1917 or on any subsequent occasion.

Great Britain was undoubtedly committed to enabling the Jews to rebuild in Palestine a 'national home," and even those who interpret that ambiguous and much-canvassed term most narrowly would admit that such cultural enterprise as the foundation of a university falls within the scope of it.

But the leaders of the Arab community in Palestine had seen it fit to make Lord Balfour's visit the occasion for hostile demonstration.

That was the worst battleground that they could have chosen for a cause, which was a strong one in some respects.

But it was even much worse in Syria and Lebanon.

Lord Balfour in Damascus: The Arab Nationalist demonstrations against Lord Balfour, which in Palestine were confined to orderly expressions of national mourning, took a much more violent form when he visited Damascus, outside the boundaries of that territory in which we stand committed, under the Balfour Declaration, to foster a Jewish national home. When Lord Balfour arrived in Damascus on Wednesday, *(April)* the 8th, *(1925),* his hotel was stoned. And he was warned not to show himself in the streets; yet, though he remained indoors, the knowledge of his presence in the city produced such a wave of hostile feeling that on Thursday all Damascus was in an uproar.

A large mob[59] made determined efforts to take the hotel by storm, and Lord Balfour's life was probably saved by the gallant conduct, at the critical moment, of a French gendarmerie officer. The police were unable to better the mob without being reinforced by the North African spahi cavalry.[60] Happily, the causalities were small – far smaller than could have been expected considering the scale of the disturbances and the degree of passion aroused – and this success, on which the French authorities deserve the warmest congratulation, was crowned by the skill with which they spirited their embarrassing visitor away to Beirut that same afternoon.

At Beirut, Lord Balfour went on board of a steamer and stayed on board until he sailed to Alexandria – very prudently, for, though Beirut is

---

[59] A mob of 5,000 strong, using sticks and stones, broke through the cordon and rushed to the hotel, driving back a small force of mounted police and French gendarmerie. An officer, lying practically full length on horseback, singly charged the crowd and broke their formation, enabling his men to rally and push back the crowd to a safe distance from the hotel [...] The civilian casualties are about 50, of whom 15 were sent to hospital, three dangerously hurt] Curtesy *Reuter* "Flight to Coast – April 11, 1925.

[60] *Spahi* is North African cavalry, migrated in the French army, recruited primarily from Morocco, Algeria and Tunisia, also include troops of Senegal origin.

the capital of the Christian Republic of Lebanon, the Christian Arabs of Syria and Palestine are no less hostile to Zionism than their Muslim fellow-nationals.

It is not recorded to which religion belonged those enthusiasts who gathered on a promontory to shout through a megaphone their denunciations of the Balfour Declaration as Lord Balfour's ship steamed out from Beirut, bound for a neighbouring *(sic)* Arab country.

There will be widespread sympathy with Lord Balfour for having suffered his painful experience. It is deplorable that the Arabs should maintain this violent and implacable opposition towards Zionism in any and every form.

The Balfour Declaration itself contains a saving clause to the effect that the establishment of the Jewish national home in Palestine is without prejudice to the civil and religious rights of existing non-Jewish communities. We have not undertaken to turn Palestine into a Jewish National State. We have never pursued a policy directed towards that end since we have administered the country, first under military occupation, and latterly under a mandate.

Therefore, we deplore this Arab intransigence, but, at the same time, we do not underestimate the gravity of the incident, which has just occurred, which is significant from two points of view.

In the first place, though agitators may have worked up the disturbances, the anti-Zionist cry is one to which the Arab population responds *en masse* with alacrity. In other words, it represents a genuine, though mistaken, national feeling.

In the second place, the fact that the outbreak occurred in Damascus underlines the artificiality of the post-war international frontier which has partitioned into a British and a French-mandated territory a group of ex-Ottoman provinces which hang together geographically, and which are inhabited by an Arab majority with a strong sense of national solidarity.

Damascus is the national capital of Greater Syria. Palestine would have been included as one of several Federal States if the Arab majority had been allowed to determine its destiny at the Peace Settlement.

This is a hard fact which does not fit into our programme *(sic)*.[61]

[61] The Economist, Saturday April 18, 1925; Pg. 747: Issue 4260.

Chapter 14.   *Armenia.*

Since 1912, the broad Eastern question and its relation to Turkey and Armenia had been on the Agenda of Russia, France, England, and Italy.

England and France declared that the Armenians' problem would never be solved until the Turkish government was wiped from the face of the earth. The people of that *benighted race* (the Armenians) were given a chance to live like other earth nations.

At that time, there was never any answer to the question: Why don't the Armenians fight for their independence as other oppressed people have done?

The answer was: The utter hopelessness of an attempt of four-millions of downtrodden Armenians to defeat twenty-five-millions of halves civilized and almost fiendish Turks who have in their hands all the power of an oppressive government and unlimited wealth at their command.

The Armenians were looking for better days ahead to right what's wrong. And they remained hopeful of a Great Power to help bail themselves out.

The time came with the great war.

And the question of Armenia remained open.

The Allies felt the heat because they had not bailed out Armenia in 1912 when Italy engaged the Ottomans. Had they done so, the Armenian massacres that began in 1915 would not have happened in such magnitude and turned into genocide.

Mark Sykes and George Picot were the living witnesses of historical tragedy. On their roadmaps, they drew dotted lines on the sands, not the high seas.

The Allied attacks on Dardanelle that commenced on March 18, 1915, resulted in the Turkish authorities arresting, in Zeitoun, many of the remaining Armenian notables and intellectuals, they tortured and finally killed. The Turks, having suspected some cooperation between the Armenians in Turkey with the advancing fleet, massacred *their* Armenian people without evidence of such 'alleged' conspiracy.

The Allies' attack was ill-fated.

There had not been a prearranged streamlining method on the British and the French forces on the sea. During the high-sea attack, friendly fires were exchanged in error, and the Allies' losses mounted. At the age of 42, Churchill had been too pushy to finish the job, and he failed.

In an article in the *Morning Post* entitled "The Dardanelles Blunder," it made Winston Churchill responsible, against the opinion of his naval adviser, for the "premature and one-sided attack, which ended disastrously on March 18, 1915, with the sinking of three battleships." According to the *Morning Post*, it was Churchill's fault that the Navy acted without military cooperation.

The British and American archives mentioned that: "Support from the rest of the British War Command came none too soon for Winston Churchill, the British First Lord of the Admiralty, who had long been a proponent of an aggressive naval assault against Turkey at the Dardanelles. Though others — especially the French military command, led by their chief, Joseph Joffre — argued that the Navy should not strike until ground troops could be spared from the Western Front, Churchill pushed to begin immediately.

The high-sea attack, planned throughout the winter of 1915, opened on March 18, 1915, when six English and four French battleships headed towards the straits."

Such chaos, on which Winston Churchill was described as "an amateur with the conduct of naval and military operations," was highly responsible for the genocide against the Armenians who had been hopeful of an Allies' breakthrough.

And Czar's Russia was weak enough to act alone.

RUSSIA IN ASIA. THE CAUCASUS.

General Situation. - Mr. Stevens telegraphed from Tiflis on the 5th of January [No. 6] that during the past few days, the general situation had become alarming in South Caucasus. Collisions, with much loss of life, were taking place between Russian soldiers returning from the front and Muslim troops, tribesmen, and Persian brigands.

A brigade of mixed nationalities was being formed at Tiflis with a view to the pacification of disturbing elements in the affected districts. It was said that Turkish military agents were agitating in various places, trying to incite a general massacre of Armenians. The news from Urumia was very disquieting. The Catholic Chaldean bishop and the Orthodox bishop had come to Tiflis to appeal for protection; they described the situation as a very grave one. According to them, Persian bandits and Turkish Kurds were combining with the object of assassinating the whole Christian population directly the Russian troops were withdrawn. This massacre, they said, could only be averted either by the presence of a strong military force or by the capture of Mosul.[62]

---

[62] The British Archives; CAB/24/144; Image Ref: 0025 of January 11, 1918.

Up to this point, America decided to stay on the sideline during the crisis. Not only was Syria looking to America for help. Armenia was also on the Jericho road - *Persian bandits and Turkish Kurds were combining with the object of assassinating the whole Christian population directly the Russian troops were withdrawn.*

On the other side, the French and the British had passed, and Armenia was looking to America as her excellent Samaritan – as a unique, helpful, and impartial nation.

It seemed likely that the road from Jerusalem to Jericho also should line up with the Samaritan and let the man on the Jericho road - Great Britain - suffer a return visit of the robbers. In the time of Jesus, the road from Jerusalem to Jericho was notorious for its danger and difficulty and was known as the "Way of Blood" because "of the blood which is often shed there by robbers."

What if the Americans do line up with the French and the British?

Suppose America should continue to hesitate to take the Armenian mandate that Armenia desires and Europe expect of the USA. In that case, America might, by her hesitation, extend the war into the unforeseeable future.

Indeed, a new world war became impending.

It turned into a battle of faiths.

The Muslim world was restive; it realized that the Christians were very wary.

Still, the Muslim world did not rise for Germany in 1915 and 1916. Germany tried *to incite* the Muslims against the Allies, but in the middle of the great war, the Muslim world became edgier. The bad feeling was predominant that promises of independence were not kept in Egypt, and other liberties were violated as to India. And doubtless, incited to this feeling by German agents - the defenders of the Muslim faith – the Germans were beginning to give unmistakable signs that they understood their position of power. "They *(The Germans)* are the only warlike people in the world at present."[63]

At that moment, the American public firmly believed that one thing could restrain the victors – namely, England and France: An American mandate in Armenia. Why Armenia? The reason is that she is the eastern outpost of the Christian faith.

The Armenians of Turkey were aware that, in 1916, the Allied Powers, Russia, France, and Great Britain, agreed in their military advance; they 'color-zoned' the lands on which the military operations were to be conducted.
Consequently, The Armenians of Turkey were made well-aware that the advancing armies had been filled with enthusiastic Muslim soldiers. In the case of victory, the colored zone or zones they so allocated were zones of influence.
The Armenians of Turkey believed the colored zones included Armenia.
But which Armenia?
That was the one bordering on the Turkish and Russian provinces. And that was the notorious Sykes-Picot roadmaps that had served the purposes of military operations in vast areas – and, now – October 1917, had nothing to recommend it to the Armenians.
It was because Czarist Russia was no more.

For some time back, it will be remembered that the reform scheme proposed by the Russian Czar at the end of 1912 expressly aimed at the establishment of European control over the six vilayets of Asiatic Turkey by limiting the right of the Porte in the appointment of the highest functionaries in these areas.
Sykes-Picot had not even been conceived.
The modified reform scheme of 1913 gave the Porte power of appointment, but not dismissal, and the

---

[63] The American Archives. The Topeka Daily Capital – Kansas, Sunday, May 11, 1919 reported by William Allen White.

Christian vilayets' administration was to be taken mostly out of Turkey's hands. Unfortunately, this scheme's benefits mainly depended upon the intention of the Porte to cooperate regarding the appointment. That intention was not forthcoming because of suspicion that the Young Turk politicians' minds aroused the reform scheme. The idea of limiting Turkish sovereignty strengthened the hands of the group led by Enver Pasha, which from that time onwards determined to settle the Armenian question on the principle of blood and iron, whenever the opportunity should arise.[64]

Again, Sykes-Picot had not been brought into existence.

Time passed quickly and swept with it many dreams turned into nightmares. Later, the roadmaps had been designed when Armenia had been, *ipso facto*, part of Russia, as Russia had been privy to Sykes-Picot's plans.

It is now Bolshevik Russia.

At that time, Armenians were still ready to support it with the one hope of getting free from Turkey.

Armenians from the United States and Egypt enrolled in the French Legion of the Orient. They fought France and the Allies' battles, under the French leadership, against the Turks in Palestine and Syria.

In ANNEX II[65] of this book, contrary to the current widespread propaganda, one can spot that – before Sykes-Picot - the rationale for the 'approach' to settling the Armenian question was also made based on Race and not only Faith.

This one is in contrast with the period that came immediately after Sykes-Picot. Suddenly, the 'approach' for having spheres of influence was portrayed to be made on Faith: Jews, Sunni, Druze, Shia, Maronites, etc., rather

---

[64] The influence of the Enver Pasha group became more and more strong all through 1913.

[65] The British Archives CAB/24/95 of December 24, 1919 Image Ref: 0037.

than Race and Culture – Aramaic, Syriac, Sam (Arabized), Kurds, Indo-Teutonic.

It is Sykes-Picot that everyone thought the Allies had wished to put through – or were doing – in the Levant and Arabia, even though one of its signatories, Russia, had dropped out of the war. The United States took its place and did much to make the victory guaranteed.

As an integral signatory, Czar's Russia's dropping-out meant that Sykes-Picot had become null and void.

As it was interpreted in France, the present British view was that with Russia's collapse, the *so-called*, Agreement including her and the Sykes-Picot 'zones', became invalid.

France disputed that in 1916 Russia, like Italy, was not an active partner to Sykes-Picot, so her collapse was not in any way a factor. The year previous, there had been an agreement concerning Turkey's future disposition in Asia made by England, France, and Russia.

Czarist Russia was to have Constantinople and allowed to push her Armenian border further west into Turkish Armenia. All had now been turned topsy-turvy after the collapse of the Russia Czardom, including Sykes-Picot.

Nevertheless, Sykes-Picot did serve Russia's aspirations for Allied Victory. But the victory had come, only after the USA had interfered in the war.

For the Americans, War and Diplomacy were intermingled like thorny cactus of the desert wild. The United States was not at war with Turkey. American troops were in Russia with whom the USA had no conflict.

The American people were ignorant of Sykes-Picot. Without Russia, Sykes-Picot had become a marginal tool. Without field battles, Sykes-Picot was not necessary.

Only the terms of the *Entente Cordiale* remained active,[66] and hence there were no pressing needs for France and England to inform the Americans about Sykes-Picot.

Belatedly, the Americans discovered that their soldiers were hardly fighting to give Cilicia and lower Armenia to France, while French diplomats were working day and night to make formal the division of Turkey on the 'dotted' lines of Sykes-Picot.

And there must have been some 'secret' words in that mishmash of uncoordinated political languages, which none of the players pronounced correctly.

By January 1918, with France's weakening – *militarily*, and the 'demise' of Czarist Russia – *physically*, and the confusions in America - *politically*, Great Britain remained the region's *active decision-maker*. England was trying 'to go for it' alone.

> *The Arab Committee:* Sir R. Wingate telegraphed on the 7th of January [No. 46] that he had received a letter from the Arab Committee in Cairo, thanking him for transmitting one from Sir Mark Sykes, which enabled them to realize that the liberation of Syria, Armenia, and the remainder of the Arab provinces were the primary consideration. They noted, too, with pleasure that the Zionists desired merely to have the right of settling in Palestine and there living their national life. They undertook to act on Sir Wingate's advice and endeavor to attain a full agreement with the Armenians and the Zionists.[67]

---

[66] The *Entente Cordiale* (April-1904) between Great Britain and France, in no sense, created an alliance and did not entangle Great Britain with a French commitment to Russia (1894). *Entente Cordiale* settled some controversial matters, ending antagonisms and paving the way for their diplomatic cooperation against German 'pressures' in the decade preceding the War (1914-19).

[67] Courtesy of The British Archives – Easter Report No. L of January 10, 1918. Incorporating Arabian Report N.S. LXXVII – Ref CAB/24/144. (Image reference 25)

Like King Feisal of Syria, the Armenians discovered that the war's most splendid and wealthiest spoils were the Turkish empire. They expected that the disposition of those enormously valuable territories should present a golden opportunity for the Old Diplomacy, and this was what the Zionists also found. Feisal, the Armenians, and the Jews (notably the Zionists) felt a remarkable group of secret treaties between France and Great Britain.

They also felt that arrangements, conversations, obscure words, being the most entangling of any, all intended to be, at the same time, by-products of the 'Old Order,' viz: *The Entente Cordiale.*

In Nov 1918, the French returned to Paris, thinking big. Many diplomats were being held in the hotels; men and women of *misty* nationality had come to France from all over the world and had been upstart diplomats. They were afraid to talk to the French politicians; they suspected each other as much as the spy catchers did.

France was afraid of England getting a significant share and too high a grip on Turkey.

Therefore, the French began negotiations with their old friends – the Russians, and at the same time planning a "showdown" with the British.

The Russians were the most miserable and unhappy lot of human beings that the post-October-1917 period had ever seen in all the war.

Armenia, being at the borders of new Russia, took the backseat. The result was another hodgepodge of secret negotiations devoted wholly to Turkey's disposal and the Armenians' detriment.

Chapter 15. *Surrounded by Foes.*

In 1919, Armenia was surrounded by enemies keen to destroy this "Christian outpost."[68]

The Muslims did not fear any severe interference from the Europeans.

Bolshevism had bound Russia; anti-imperialism in the labor party had weakened the strong arm of England.

France was decrepit and could wage no war for purely financial reasons, if for no others.

America still was strong.
The United States had plenty of enthusiasts and sufficient power to back her enthusiasm. If she established a protectorate in Armenia, the eastern outpost of Christianity would be safe without striking a blow.
The American missionaries, who came with the Bible in one hand, and the excellent educational systems in the other, laid the foundation of a lot of good things, including pragmatic business enterprises.
Many Americans conversant with the former Ottoman Empire, and its surroundings were hopeful that their country would eventually take the Mandate over Syria (including Palestine and Lebanon) and Armenia.
They feared that America might take it only after another war had started and after a further effort had made it necessary.

---

[68] "Christian outpost," is the term used in the American Archives, and mentioned, several times, in newspapers published in the USA.

A watchful waiting policy then meant the beginning of a second phase of the 'modern' thirty years' war. It was not even coming in thirty years.

The hopes had been enough high of active American interference in the provinces of the former Ottoman Empire.

When the American peace delegation came to Paris, the American newspapermen became acquainted with a man somewhat over 70 years of age. He was a curious figure, short, with extensive shoulders and a massive chest and a large head; he was well known to all the prominent European statesmen but unknown to most Americans.

His one desire was to meet the statesmen of the vast republic of the West, in whose power and altruism he and his people had absolute and childlike faith.

His one wish was to present his people before the American statesmen, in the supreme belief that this would save his people – the Armenian nation.

The figure was Boghos Nubar Pasha, son of Armenian Nubar Pasha, the prime minister of Egypt under Lord Cromer. At present, Boghos was the Armenian delegation president, representing the Armenian people throughout the world.

Boghos Nubar Pasha had been a lifelong friend of Clemenceau and well known to Balfour. It was difficult for him to obtain an audience with the United States representatives because they were busied with the League of Nations.

It would have been disrespectful to talk to the Americans without synchronizing with his friends, the British, and the French. Boghos Pasha didn't know that the two great powers were, currently, at loggerheads.

In this situation, both Powers regarded as a more significant challenge, now, their people's welfare, not others'.

When the Russian Revolution broke out in October 1917, the old regime's Russian armies had gradually melted away before the Turkish advance; they withdrew from the Turkish-Armenian provinces northward into Russian Armenia, where their forces dissolved. In their retreat, several hundred thousand refugees from Turkish Armenia went into the Armenian regions of Transcaucasia[69] in Russia, fleeing the certainty of death at the Turkish and Kurdish bands' hands. These refugees were still living among the Armenian relatives of the north. Daily they died by hundreds of disease and starvation, despite the significant efforts of the organized expeditions of the Armenian and Syrian relief of the Red Cross and the charitable organizations.

In January 1919, another delegation arrived, a group of intelligent and virile men from Transcaucasia Armenia headed by Avetis Aharonian, formerly president of the newly constituted Armenian Republic of Transcaucasia. He resigned this office to represent his section of the Armenian people at the Peace Conference in Paris on January 12, 1919.

On February 26, Boghos Nubar Pasha and Avetis Aharonian were called before the higher council of ten of the conference to explain the Armenians' demands. The desires of all the Armenians were the same:
That Armenia is freed from Turkish misrule.
The Armenian state should include Adana's vilayet, which comprises most of the ancient Armenian Kingdom of Cilicia.[70]

---

[69] Transcaucasia or the South Caucasus, is a geopolitical region near the southern Caucasus Mountains on the border of Eastern Europe and Western Asia. Transcaucasia roughly corresponds to modern Georgia, Armenia, and Azerbaijan.

[70] In antiquity, Cilicia was the south coastal region of Asia Minor and existed as a political entity from Hittite times into the Armenian Kingdom of Cilicia during the late Byzantine Empire.

And that all the Armenians, both those of the old Russian Empire in Transcaucasia and those of Turkey, should be united in one state and under one regime.

Privately they desired American Mandate but dared not ask it. For if it were refused, the Armenians would suffer from presenting this claim.

Judged by the standards of unnecessary suffering at the hands of the Young Turk government during the war, and by the adherence to the Allied cause against odds which would have driven a people less tenacious into any deal, however ignoble with the enemy, the case of the Armenians stood beside that of Belgium. The horror of their sufferings had been infinitely more significant than that of the Belgians.

But, in 1919, the French and the British had nothing else to refer to. In the armistice with Turkey, Armenia was not occupied by Allied troops. No provision was made for evacuation by forces led by the Young Turk Organization's brutal officers. England and France were in a hurry. And they believed the USA had delivered what was required of her; now it was time to *tell* the Americans "Thank You Very Much."

If the Americans had declined a Mandate over Armenia, they would do the same toward the Levant and Arabia.

If Wilson's points, which were in no way a detailed program, had been adopted as the general basis of future political arrangements in the early days of the war, it would indeed have been possible to turn the Sykes-Picot *military* roadmaps into a *political* instrument.

If this had happened, mighty America would have been accused of conspiring to create the Levantine confusion of 1919 – of mixing between urgently needed *military* roadmaps and *political* arrangements for the future.

France pressed to cut off the lower Armenian districts and Cilicia from the northern Armenian areas of the old Turkish Empire and the Armenians in Transcaucasia.

Neither by geographic definition, nor on economic grounds, nor by ethnic distribution, do Cilicia and lower Armenia belonged in "Syria," as the French claimed they did.

France's appetite was open to swallow entire Syria, inclusive of the lower Armenian districts. Here, France had been banking on the Sykes-Picot *Treaty.* '

But nothing of all the above had had any links with the roadmaps of Sykes-Picot.

All the above had just come on the spur of the moment and during marginal discussions behind closed doors.

It was not fair; Armenia was not a minimal rental property. The Armenian blood was spilled for a just cause and was destined to bear fruit.

It was firmly believed that the general situation in the Levant would determine the destiny of the Armenians.

The situation in 1919 was that the old Turkish tyrannical rule was removed. Just as the removal of the hard hand of the former Russian regime resulted in chaos in the Russian Empire, so the breaking down of Turkey would naturally lead to turmoil in the Ottoman Empire – but one fact:

Certain areas, Palestine, Syria, and Mesopotamia, were firmly held by Allied forces.

British troops had occupied the railway centers, Baku, Tiflis, Batik, Kars, Alexandropoulos in Transcaucasia. French troops, chiefly the Armenians of the French Legion of the Orient, occupied Cilicia's principal cities.

The French felt they didn't have to look to the future for a cause for anxiety. The present condition was bad enough. The British refused to leave what France believed to be the French zone. Even the British sent away French troops that existed in the regions in dispute as Adana and elsewhere in Cilicia, which might have come under the American Mandate for Armenia.

This Allied occupation was too thin to be effective, except in Syria, Palestine, and Mesopotamia.

The revolt that was going on in Egypt was primarily a nationalistic Egyptian movement, but it had in it, also, something of the Muslim feeling against the Christian world.

Only so could the killing of Armenians in Cairo be explained. If there were an anti-western outbreak in the nearer-Orient, its victims would be the Armenian race's remnants. "For they are the eastern outposts of the "Christian world."

In 1919, the Armenians were living amongst the Muslim Turks, and where they lived in small groups, were wedged in between the Turks, the Tartars on the north-east, the Muslims of Persia to the East, and the Arab-Muslim world to the south.

And some Turks didn't like having the Armenians and the Americans working for a hand in glove.

The advocates of an American Mandate over the entire Turkish Empire were divided into three groups.

First: those Turks, intelligent enough to see that their empire could be saved to themselves by only in one way – an American Mandate over the entire empire.

They hoped to see the United States play now the role that saved the Turkish Empire from disruption, which England had played in the Crimean War, some seventy years before.

Second: individual financial interests that found a more significant opportunity to exploit the natural resources of the former Ottoman Empire, undivided into its component's parts.

Third: missionaries and philanthropists who were interested in religious and relief work in the Near East.

The first two groups were composed of intelligent men and women actuated by self-interest, who knew what they wanted. Their opinions, however, would not carry weight with the American public in its decision on the question of a mandate.

The views of the men and women of the last group would take comparatively more weight because they were known in the United States as authorities on Near East questions. These people were carried away by enthusiasm for the excellent work they were doing and were losing sight of some crucial facts pertinent to the issue of an American mandate.

They wanted to conduct religious and philanthropic work on a large scale in the Near East and were anxious for their operations' vast and undivided field.

The Americans did not forget or ignore the feelings and aspirations of the people they wished to help.

They realized that the orphans and widows they would have saved from starvation would turn against their rescuers when they learned that these rescuers were also instrumental in yoking their destinies once more to their traditional enemy oppressors.

Any mandates honestly undertaken could have only one object – to render the people under the mandate self-governing within an exact number of years. The object could not be achieved by any mandate that aims to bind together such *incompatible elements* as Turks and Armenians; Greeks and Kurds; Syrians and Fellahin. Even each of the *races* oppressed by the Turks lacked national aspirations; it would take several generations of the most careful supervision to enable them to forget the horrible crimes committed against them and produce the community feeling necessary for a stable form of self-government.

But each of the principal *races* of Turkey has clung for centuries to the ideal of national independence and cannot be induced to relinquish it for any settlement which is not in harmony with this ideal. Here lies the great difficulty in the Near Eastern question.

There is only one correct solution to the problem – the final liquidation of the Turkish Empire. This involves not only the *breaking down* of the empire into its components parts, as in the case of the late Austro-Hungarian Empire, but a transplanting and regrouping of the *members of the different races* to make the population of each geographical unit a reasonably homogeneous mass.[71]

That was the prevailing thinking, with or without Sykes-Picot.
In the Levant, Syria's problem, the position, and the future of the Arab States, the future relations between France and Britain had been raised as matters of urgency.
It was suggested that a comprehensive settlement could be worked out now for these problems.
And Sykes-Picot's roadmaps had been readily available without any government of the two Powers having a sufficiently clear picture of its future policy in the Levant, Armenia, or Arabia, to prevent decisions from being taken now which might prejudice solutions in the future.

---

[71] Refer to 'Reasons Why America Should Not Attempt to perpetuate the Unity of the Turkish Empire,' by H. M. Dadourian, Ph. D. – Courtesy of the American Archives and the New York Times of Friday, October 17, 1919.

Chapter 16. *"The Sick Man of America."*

Of course, American troops played a significant part in the great victory.

The capture of Sedan will go down in history as one of the most brilliant achievements of this war, and it left the German army bottled up, with only one avenue of escape, through Liege.

Everybody agreed that Germany unconditionally surrendered because it had been beaten to its knees by the Allied armies.

Everyone believed that the days of the Prussian *swashbuckler* were forever over.

The Treaty of Versailles (French: *Traité de Versailles*) was one of the peace treaties at the end of World War I. It ended the state of war between Germany and the Allied Powers. It was signed on 28 June 1919, exactly five years after the assassination of Archduke Franz Ferdinand.

The Treaty of Versailles created nine new nations:
Finland, Austria, Czechoslovakia, Yugoslavia, Poland, Hungary, Latvia, Lithuania, and Estonia.

Thus, the former empire of Austria-Hungary was dissolved. Of course, here, there was no Sykes-Picot on which to fall to rationalize such arrangements in Europe.

The Treaty of Versailles punished Germany by taking away territories and overseas colonies, reducing the nation's army's size, and forcing Germany to pay reparations.

Mostly, Germany was compelled to take the blame for World War.

Presented for German leaders to sign on May 7, 1919, the treaty forced Germany to concede territories to Belgium (Eupen-Malmédy), Czechoslovakia (the Hultschin district), and Poland (Poznan [German: Posen], West Prussia, and Upper Silesia).

Also, and here is one *small* example of the financial penalties:
Advances made to Belgium by France, America, and England had been,

> "annulled by the Treaty of Versailles. This Burden of debt had been 'transferred to Germany's shoulders by the following clause in Article 232 of the Treaty:
>
> Germany undertakes [...] to reimburse all sums which Belgium has borrowed from the Allied and Associated Governments up to November 11, 1918, together with interest at the rate of 5 percent per annum on such sums.
>
> This amount shall be determined by the Reparation Commission, and the German Government undertakes thereupon forthwith to make a special issue of bearer bonds to an equivalent amount payable in marks of gold, on May 1, 1926, or at the option of the German Government on May 1st in any year up to 1926."
>
> At a par of exchange, British pre-Armistice advances to Belgium amounted to about seventy-five million sterling pounds. In his last Budget speech, Chamberlain gave total advances to Belgium as eighty-seven million sterling pounds [...][72]

---

[72] *The Economist*, November 1, 1919; Page 808, Issue 3975 *(Excerpts)*

Of course, the Ottoman Turks had to give up much of their land in southwest Asia and the Middle East.

In Europe, they retained only the country of Turkey.

Nevertheless, the Treaty of Versailles did not mention anything about Sykes-Picot.

The scrutiny, debates, and implementation were all left to France and England's friendly enemies.

Yes, it was a military victory by some and a military defeat by others, but also, it was a political failure by all to all.

By 1920, the Turks' challenge was to answer an ultimatum from the Supreme Council of the Allies at Spa that Turkey must sign the Peace Treaty or leave Europe.

The Turks' real defeat increased their sense of defiance, but for the Arabs' regions in which Sykes-Picot had tried to assemble like colleagues to serve the Allies' war aims, it was something else. And the faults of the Arabs and Levantine cannot be denied or ignored.

By 1920, like always, the Arab and Levantine clans, families, warlords, feudal, remained divided, while running pell-mell - and encouraged by the British - espousing Pan-Arabism.

Most of the areas under Sykes-Picot were the wildland of extreme poverty.

It was also a land of factions and vendettas.

Their divisions were in sectarian denominations', tribalism, and blood feuds, as post-war European countries and the United States were keen on areas – with lowest densities of the population - much more significant than many European states had ever dreamed of having.

By her soft diplomacy and cunning, England was able to keep pace with both – the sectarian denominations and the tribalism (in the remote areas) and the Pan-Arabism, (notably in the cities.)

_____

(£87 million in 1920 is equivalent to four billion in 2017)

By 1920, one of the international issues confronting the people of Europe and the United States was whether the longtime "Sick Man of Europe" shall be accepted in effect as the "Sick Man of America."

But things changed for the worse for the European population.

As France's Georges Clemenceau became the spokesperson of Europe, the world discovered how French diplomacy could fail in taming the Arabs.

The world was surprised to find out how the "unshakable Turk" was driven from Europe by the inevitable results of the First World War, and how far, in Arabia, the seeds for "Clannishness and Cliquishness traditions" fell on fertile ground.

Diplomatic failure, followed by the financial crash indicators, warring Europe, was now rejected, in essence, as the "Sick Man of America."

By 1920, the challenges for the Armenian people were to remain united.

The time of trial was coming sooner than expected.

The Armenian Holocaust (1915-1917 and prior) exterminated 1.5 million inhabitants, and their current plight troubled most of Europe, but it merely elicited lip service.

Europe's silence and reticence to rise in the Turks' face overwhelmed the Armenian plight with pain, grief, and humiliation. But the very isolation of the Armenians strengthened their identity.

The Armenian fires enraged the Americans, who were expecting further trouble to brew.

For the Europeans, the pressure of failure to rescue the Armenians was unbearable.

It was all an appalling misjudgment.

Instead of peace coming to the region, the aftermath of the war atrocities still poisoned the entire area.

The Armenians' fate decided that a new ideology was poised to take center stage – the Bolsheviks.
Such burgeoning, but still soft power, required a grown-up and still whole nation to check it – the US.
But Woodrow Wilson didn't care much about WWI booty and decided what the former Ottoman Empire needed most was less American involvement than more.

By 1920, Woodrow Wilson was already getting disenchanted with the European leaders – notably the French - because of their stubbornness over the costs of German reparations, the ill-fated Armenians, and the split-up of the 'Turkish booty.'

The American president had been in a sad state of confusion with the European leaders; his sudden decision to withdraw had left them puzzled but relieved.
The breakdown of trust between himself and Lloyd George, Vittorio Orlando, and in particular, his mistrust of George Clemenceau, was another appalling assessment that was to mark the American policy of isolationism.

Chapter 17. *"...a controversy over the Coffin..."*

When Georges Clemenceau died in 1929, at the age of 88, Mark Sykes had been dead for about ten years.

Little the Levant people heard of Mark Sykes, but they understood much about Georges Picot and Georges Clemenceau. However, the former had been acting behind the stage until the war ended, and the peace negotiations began.

Clemenceau had been the real power behind the interpretation of Sykes-Picot as a *Treaty* - a political instrument - throughout his leadership, notably, since he had been France's Prime Minister and Minister of War from 1917 to 1920.

Georges Benjamin Clemenceau was labeled 'The Tiger;' some preferred to call him "Godfather.'

Hope for his recovery had long been abandoned.

The Tiger, the cynical philosopher as he was, clung to life as the uremic poison crept slowly through his system.

He died in a big bed with a dragon carved on the headboard and other monsters at the foot.

In his moment of clarity, he showed himself grimly determined to have his way to the last.

A long procession of visitors, including French political and cultural life leaders, called at his apartment to leave their cards.

Hundreds stood in the streets outside.

It was rumored that, like his father, Clemenceau probably would be buried in an upright position.

The elder Clemenceau was of stern stuff, authoritative and dominating. The Tiger inherited his father's dictatorial position in Vendée province, an agricultural region that was the scene of a high Royalists' uprising during the French Revolution. He often was called upon to arbitrate disputes between peasants. And so, the Tiger did the same, but in creating - and later mediating - conflicts between nations. Except that the disputes were mainly of his making.

The Tiger was a physician himself and was under no illusions that the span of his life had been measured for several months. He felt the end approaching and even told friends that he would die this year - 1929.

Like Napoleon Bonaparte, the Tiger believed that history is "a set of lies agreed upon."

In 1870, when the power of Napoleon III was waning rapidly, Clemenceau returned to France.

Throughout the Franco-Prussian war and the siege of Paris, he was mayor of the Montmartre district. He was first elected to the General Assembly in 1871, five years later, to the Chamber of Deputies, where he soon became a leader of the radicals.

The Tiger, then, was disgraced. He was accused of complicity in the Panama Canal scandal.[73] While he met every charge against his integrity, the attacks on him in the Chamber broke him down entirely as his constituents turned against him. For nine years, he had no connection with the government of France.

Clemenceau's associations with the Jewish financier Cornélius Herz, who was deeply involved in the Panama affair, inevitably threw suspicion on him; later, the banker was accused of being in the British Foreign Office pay.

The attack on Clemenceau was mounted in the daily newspaper, *Le Petit Journal;* it took a dramatic turn when, in the Chamber of Deputies on December 20, 1892,

---

[73] The Panama scandals was a corruption affair that broke out in the French Third Republic in 1892, linked to the building of the Panama Canal. Close to a billion francs were lost when the French Government took bribes to keep quiet about the Panama Canal Company's financial troubles.

the author and Boulangist Paul Déroulède denounced him as the protégé and supporter of Herz.

Clemenceau claimed that Déroulède was lying and challenged him to a duel, in which neither was hurt. More actually, Clemenceau brought a successful lawsuit against his detractors. Their condemnation forced some of them to resign as deputies, but they took Clemenceau with them in the end.

All the accumulated venom he had aroused was concentrated in the election of 1893 when, standing again for *Le Var département – in the Provence-Alps-Cote d'Azur – in southern France,* Clemenceau was attacked on all sides. Despite conducting an exhaustive and brilliant campaign, he was defeated but never demoralized.

Clemenceau tried his hand at writing a play. However, he was mostly a journalist and inevitably wrote much about the Dreyfus case, which agitated France from 1894 to 1906.

At first, Clemenceau had assumed that the young Jewish officer Alfred Dreyfus had, indeed, been guilty of selling secrets to Germany. The Tiger's hatred for the Germans was like a man ready to burn his house to get rid of a rat. Nevertheless, once convinced of Dreyfus's innocence, Clemenceau carried on an eight-year battle (1897–1905) in his newspapers "La *Justice* and *L'Aurore*" (founded in 1897). He wished to bother his rivals without worrying about his country.

Clemenceau's support for Dreyfus brought him back into favor with his fellow Republicans, and he was prevailed upon to accept election as a senator for *Le Var* in April 1902.

Georges Benjamin Clemenceau was an adamant Anti-Clerical, but his ruling in one of these cases was the parish priest against a countess who insisted on bringing her dogs to mass on Sundays. The Tiger obliged her to keep her dogs at home.

His hate of the clerics stems from his observation of the Russian Rasputin, a man who could have been a good priest was playing God.

However, the man was a chameleon. Like the lizard of Africa, Georges Clemenceau was able to 'change skin color, having a projectile tongue like a snake.'

It would have been better if Clemenceau had remained secular. But instead, he changed color when he insisted that the Maronites in Lebanon would have an authoritative role in the ruling of Greater Lebanon. In his strategic mind, he realized that the Muslims would outnumber the Christians by higher birth rates, and hence the Christians would always revert to France for 'protection.'

As an atheist, the Tiger intended to put God to work for his politics and maximize his country's potential – France. Georges Clemenceau was France, and France was Georges Clemenceau.

Death found Georges Clemenceau battling with the sharpest of pens against what he considered unjustified attacks upon some of his actions while he was premier of France during the war.

His doctors said that overwork on his book refuting criticism attributed to the late Marshal Foch, shortened his life by many months. The Tiger had been spending six and seven hours daily at his desk through the summer and fall, and for a man nearly 90 years old, the labor proved too much.

Mutinous to the end, Clemenceau refused to obey his doctors' pleas that he takes a rest.

The first part of his memoirs had already appeared, and two volumes, *"Au Soir de la Pensée"* – In the Evening of Thought – had been published in English.

Doctor Laubry, a heart specialist, one of the dead statesman's closest personal friends, shook his head over his patient. "That book will play him a trick yet," he said.

The public first learned that there was a controversy when Raymond Recouly, a Paris journalist, and author, issued a book accepted as Foch, himself, had inspired.

The marshal even dictated parts of it, and the entire work was reviewed and corrected by him in proof before it was published.

The book came out a few days after Foch's death in the spring of 1929. It contained many criticisms of the Tiger's activities as wartime premier. One dealt with his alleged efforts to secure the removal of General John J. Pershing as Commander-in-Chief of the A. E. F [American Expeditionary Force]. Another with attempts to have the American troops incorporated with the French armies.

Clemenceau announced with characteristic vigor when Recouly's book appeared: "I hate to start a controversy over the coffin, but I am being attacked. I shall defend myself and write a book of my own." The body of Marshal Foch was lying in state at that time.

Thus, since April 1929, the Tiger worked diligently and daily with his old quill pen, whether living in his modest Paris home in the Rue Franklin or the solitary villa in Vendee, where he spent his summertime. His doctors felt all along that he was working too strenuously. But meanwhile, the book was progressing.

His book was one of his final cares; the doctors said that his 'war' – the controversy that he hated to start 'over a coffin,' had much to do with prematurely opening the Tiger's coffin.

Enough is said about his death, now back to the time he was living.

"[...] Georges Clemenceau's public career covered the span, not of one generation of ordinary men, but two. And though the chapters into which it naturally falls do not correspond with the limits of two equal generations, it remains true that the Clemenceau familiar to the Frenchman or the foreigner of yesterday was a very different figure from the Clemenceau of the Commune, the Clemenceau of the Boulanger episode, or the stormy petrel of domestic politics who set the destruction of eighteen Ministries to his credit before he became himself the personification of national unity, *l'union sacrée*, in the face of the invader of 1917."[74]

Although Clemenceau retired from active participation in French politics in 1919, after his defeat for the republic's presidency, he did not regard his life's activities finished, notwithstanding that he was then 78 years old. Later disclosed that he had planned work, which would take fifteen years to complete.

The Tiger was 76 when he was called to pilot France through the world's war darkest days. For first, he had been a bitter critic of the government in signed articles in *l'Homme Libre,* a daily newspaper established at the beginning of the war for that purpose.
He considered Germany the 'enemy' of France and possessed the will to destroy 'him.'
All other 'evil' he regarded as nothing compared with surrender to Germany.
Shortly after Clemenceau's rise to power, he caused the arrest of his former political colleague, Joseph Caillaux, on charges of commerce with the enemy – Germany – and high treason. Caillaux was convicted on the previous charges, but that of betrayal was quashed. Of the incident, Clemenceau said;

---

[74] *The Economist,* November 30,1929, Page 1008, Issue 4501
(Excerpts)

It was a case of Caillaux or myself. Poincaré had no alternative, either call Caillaux to power or call me. He chose me. Had he sent for Caillaux, the latter would have had me arrested and made peace with Germany? I decided to have Caillaux arrested and go on with the war.[75]

Clemenceau found opposition to his government as bitter as that he directed against his predecessors. He was called upon to resign in June 1918, after the Germans had broken through at Chemin des Dames, crossed the Marne, and was at Chateau-Thierry, forty miles from Paris. His answer was, "One must know what one wants; when he wants it, he must have the courage to say it and, having said it, courage enough to do it. I'll see this war through to the finish."

After he had refused the Austrian peace overtures, the furious socialists demanded: What are your aims? While pacing the speaker's tribute, like a weather-beaten old skipper on the bridge of his ship in a gale, the premier waited for the noise to abate. "Victory," he thundered at his tormentors. In the real Clemenceau characteristic manner, the one word delivered had the desired effect, and 500 deputies arose and gave him an ovation.[76]

During his administration as war premier, Clemenceau carried on his work with the same remarkable energy that characterized his life throughout his fifty years of public activity. He visited the battlefronts to get firsthand knowledge of the situation. On those occasions, he again displayed his remarkable courage and fearlessness.
On a visit to Verdun, officers from general headquarters insisted that he wear a steel helmet.

---

[75] Clemenceau's Memoirs.

[76] -Ibid-

"No," replied the Tiger, "steel helmets are the privilege of the president of the republic. I'll stick to my felt hat."

While visiting Verdun for the second time with shells exploding all around, the officer accompanying Clemenceau suggested that he lie flat upon the ground until the flurry passed. The Tiger pointing to the soldier nearby and trying to stretch himself a little more than his full height, asked: "What would you think?" "But you might be killed," the officer insisted. "It is suicide."

"Suicide! perhaps," replied the Tiger. "Suicide for love at my age, for love of France." And he continued, "France was saved three times during the war. Three great names will go down in history and live forever: The Marne, Verdun, and Clemenceau." What about Foch?" he was asked. "There should have been no need for Foch or any allied military leader in 1918," he replied.

Astonishingly enough, the appointment of Marshal Foch to command the French armies was one of the first moves of Clemenceau after assuming power, and this, in turn, led to Foch's selection as generalissimo of the entire allied forces.

Henri Poincaré, who was president of France, always followed the officers' advice regarding the steel helmet. Although it was Poincaré who called Clemenceau to form the ministry during the war, the premier never missed an opportunity to direct one of his caustic remarks at the president. However, they reconciled at the Armistice's time and shook hands when the French army entered Strasbourg.

That was in 1917, French fortunes were at a low ebb, and Clemenceau was 76.

With the war over and the German empire crushed, the Tiger rose to an equally high point during the Peace Conference in Paris, of which, as president, he was the foremost figure in the open sessions, ruling with an iron hand.

At the same time, he was one of the dominating influences of the "Big Four" – Woodrow Wilson, Lloyd George, Georges Clemenceau, and Vittorio Orlando – who held long-secret sessions shaping the work of the public assemblies and the entire universe.

The Tiger always meant that his beloved France had escaped the murder Germany planned for her and that if France still maintained an adequate army, it was because to disarm at present would be to invite German revenge – in other words, suicide for France.

> "France is not imperialist, not militarist," he said. "France is not a nation of fools, and only fools would want to burden their country with militarism. I am going to America in November to tell America so.
>
> No one has spoken for France, so I determined unofficially to cross the ocean in my old age and do so.
>
> It is one of the last and best services I can render my country. I shall present no apology. France needs none! I shall present no defense. France requires none! I shall ask nothing for France. I shall give the facts about Europe and let the Americans draw their conclusions, and determine whether they should do anything, and what they should do. It may necessitate plain talk."[77]

That was an epigram The Tiger had mentioned, in October 1922, to journalist Milton Bronner: "France escaped murder, she will not now commit suicide," summing up French history in 1914.

---

[77] The American Archives ... Wausau Daily Record Herald – Wisconsin, November 1, 1922.

The Tiger discovered that no European country could dispense with supports from America, the nation that he, himself, did his utmost to oust from the peace talks, three years before.

In 1922, as the situation developed, it became apparent that the three nations which had united to defeat Germany - namely Britain, America, and France, were poles apart. Britain soon realized that the efforts to collect an indemnity would damage her interests.

America, in advance, resigned all claims upon war payment. Still, France, where the real devastations had taken place, found herself with the alternative between bankruptcy and receipt of sufficient German reparation to meet the reconstruction cost.

This epigram had been a complete departure from the Tiger's attitude, and wit-measuring, at Versailles.

Until his death, the hanging dotted lines and gaily colored roadmaps of Sykes-Picot, cast hovering shadows on Clemenceau.

Like his dislike of Marshal Foch, Clemenceau thanked his good stars that he has never had a deep understanding and sympathy with Georges Picot or acquired any contact with Mark Sykes.

However, the roadmaps drawn by Sykes-Picot were indeed one of the most significant assets of the Allied cause in the evolution, first of the Versailles Military Council and later of a unified command.

Chapter 18. *Clemenceau: Unpredictable Quick Wit*

During the conference at Versailles, the Tiger frequently measured his humor and ability against President Woodrow Wilson, who, astonishingly enough, had nominated the Tiger to preside over the conference. Clemenceau's sarcastic remarks became most noticeable in the discussions over the so-called "Balance of Power," Clemenceau having declared his purpose of supporting the old Bismarckian policy of grouping one set of nations against another, notwithstanding the American president's opposition.

Clemenceau's unwavering determination to regard Sykes-Picot roadmaps as a binding agreement "still valid after the end of war hostilities" signed the death warrant of the victors' dreams of inheriting the Ottoman Empire and of European imperialism in general.

Clemenceau's adamancy prompted two ideologically controverted warlords – David Lloyd George, and Vladimir Lenin, to oppose him, and Woodrow Wilson to give him mental agonies until his last days.

Militarily, Sykes-Picot was a smooth-running instrument during the war operations, but diplomatically, it turned the military advantages on its head. Clemenceau turned it into an ego - his ego. The different interpretations of the purpose of Sykes-Picot, the festering soul which burst in Wilson's mind, were not over even in the presence of the new, and unpredictable, Russia.

Indeed, it was Clemenceau's final act of mental duel between himself, on the one hand, and Lloyd George and Woodrow Wilson, on the other, in which each man plotted to impose his will on the future of the Levant, Arabia, and the Middle East.

Clemenceau tried but failed to convince the other Powers to come under his direction and avoid having a say in his misinterpretation of Sykes-Picot. He hated to hear the name: Mark Sykes and endeavored to keep Georges Picot out of sight.

As the duel progressed, Wilson abandoned the arena, but his country didn't stop plotting behind France and England's back. Eventually, America would become the pivotal nation upon whom the outcome of the duel would depend. At stake was the future freedom and independence of millions of people of the former Ottoman Empire.

By Britain's interpretation that Sykes-Picot had been null and void after the war, the Anglo-Saxons tried to brush off Clemenceau, who had no clue he would be excluded. The Tiger not only felt betrayed, but he could also sense the blow to France's power. For the moment, he was mocked; beyond deceit for power-play, the disturbing one-sided British interpretation of Sykes-Picot left Clemenceau with further troubling thought. Up until now, both he and Lloyd George had handled Wilson with kid-gloves, but Clemenceau was becoming split-minded.

On one side, believing he was a great man who could deal with Wilson - another great man - by direct diplomacy. But the British interpretation of Sykes-Picot and Wilson's misunderstanding of its constant reconfiguration has awakened in Clemenceau all the old fears that the Anglo-Saxons – Britain and America - had been playing tricks behind his back.

In Paris, Clemenceau celebrated his victory over the 'most hated' Germans. But all political contestants knew that behind Versailles was violent disputes that remained unresolved.

By trying to 'outwit' the Americans, the French had lost the mind-game. The differences over land acquisition and sphere of influences created strategic and policy errors, for which France had to be responsible. Clemenceau thought of himself as the greatest politician in history. In Washington and Rome, the Americans and the Italians felt isolated. Woodrow Wilson stood aloof. Everything in the relations of the four victors - France, England, Italy, and the US – was changing in ways that seemed unimaginable five years after the Soviets took over Russia.

It looked like the Allied nations had fought a war of new empire-building, while the 'modern' Russia preferred a Peace of the Mind.

At times, Clemenceau and Lloyd George led the Americans to believe that post-war 'arrangements' had been all some private business full of the psychological duel in which Wilson felt they lied, intrigued, delighted, flattered, and conspired to be exclusive and to win it all.

To the American president, the Peace Agreement was two delusions.

First that France and Britain trusted they had won the war by themselves.

Second, the British were putting hope for a change in German 'imperial characteristics and acquisitive instincts,' which ought to bring about a 'marriage of convenience' between Germany and England to 'contain' the new Russia from building a new totalitarian empire.

This sharp division ran through the entire proceedings, leading up to creating the League of Nations, the Peace Treaty and the Joint Defensive Agreement among France, England, and the United States.

In shaping the Peace Treaty, the Tiger stood for harsh terms, which would compensate France for her sacrifice, and it was mostly through his insistence that France obtained the vast Sarre coal fields and a large part of the reparations.

And what he managed to *'devour'* in the tidy Hall of Mirrors at Versailles, he would equally devour in the Levant and Arabia from the untidy and dusty Roadmaps.

To Clemenceau, Sykes-Picot was of strategic importance to the Levant and the Arab world.

On his views about Sykes-Picot and the German reparation, the French statesman had been depicted to President Wilson as a "real tiger," ferocious and brutal, with whom it would be challenging to deal. When the facts convinced Clemenceau that Sykes-Picot was only a temporary 'arrangement' based on the battlefields' emergencies, he ignored them. He hated to see that someone he knew – George Picot, or heard of - Mark Sykes – had turned out badly after all, while he was in charge. Here is where Clemenceau's cruel and implacable nature showed itself; the past ceased to exist for him; years of friendship and fighting side-by-side with the British for 'common cause' might as well have never been.

"Well, here is a tiger who appears to be much easier to tame than most his compatriots imagine. I don't know whether he believes in the League of Nations, but he acts already as if he did. That's the principal thing. Perhaps, after a while, serving as if he believed in it, he would become a stauncher supporter of the League than I am myself," said Wilson.

During the Peace Conference, Clemenceau was dangerously wounded by an anarchist, who made a dramatic attempt to assassinate him. When the would-be-assassin, Emile Cotin, was sentenced to death for his attack on the premier's life, the old statesman recommended that the punishment is changed to imprisonment. "How long shall we give him?" asked the minister of justice. "About ten years," replied Clemenceau. "I'll be dead and gone before he comes out in case he should like to use one for a target again."

During the Peace Conference, Clemenceau was challenged, halted, and turned back by an American doughboy. The Tiger's appearance did not correspond with the mental picture of him that the American soldier had.

As the Peace Conference president, Clemenceau seeking 'Colonel House' of the American delegation to discuss a point, hiked up to the Hotel Carillon's first floor without the formality of being announced. As the Tiger reached the door to 'Colonel House's' room, he was refused admittance by the doughboy. "But I am Clemenceau, the prime minister of France," the statesman said in perfect English and with a show of impatience. "Tell that to the Marines; don't hand me that kind of bunk," the sentry was said to have replied, not unkindly, but firmly.

Clemenceau retraced his steps to the ground floor; after relating his experience to the officer of the day, he was escorted to 'Colonel House's' room. "Didn't you recognize Mr. Clemenceau, the Premier of France?" the captain asked the guard. "How could I guess?" replied the soldier. "They told me Mr. Clemenceau was 77 years of age."

At times, one could find him pragmatic and irrational, an idealist or escapist, dogmatist, and propagandist. The Tiger was a mixture of everything and thought of himself the champion of post-war Sykes-Picot as if Mark Sykes and George Picot had never existed. He treated Sykes-Picot as his private household, his first and second wife, and America his backyard. Most of his fellows could talk for hours together about the awful experience they had struck, the bad times they spent since his fate betrayed him, and pulled them down with him.

After the Treaty of Versailles had been signed, Clemenceau lost much of his opportunity. His ministry fell, and he dropped out of politics for good, but he did not drop out of public life. For a man of his reputation and his dynamic, forceful activity, that would have been impossible.

He made speeches, wrote articles, and continued as the active power to be reckoned with in French affairs.

In 1922, he went to America on a special goodwill mission, attempting - somewhat vainly – to head the rapidly growing rift between former Allies. Then he returned to La Vendee to rest in seclusion in his seacoast cottage, chew his mustache, eat large quantities of his favorite gastronomic combination – onion soup and hard-boiled eggs – and plan confusion for his critics. And he maintained his spirit of 'cooking' intrigue until the last breath. His principal one was the French's limitary intrigue to encourage a rebellion in the Rhine provinces and secure by a *coup d'etat* what they had not succeeded in getting at the Peace Conference.

When the end came, mourning his friend's death, General John J. Pershing said he regarded Georges Benjamin Clemenceau as the "outstanding world war figure among the French people."

The former British premier, David Lloyd George, was quoted as having said of the Tiger, "What an unusual, extraordinary and terrible old man. Every time I meet him, he appears to be a year younger and to have one more tooth." Some say Lloyd-George called it "One more claw." Until his last breath, The Tiger never liked the Germans. He loved to hate them. He disliked their character and characteristics. He regarded the Germans' business as keeping everyone out of business unless they needed their rivals' aid. And that's exactly how the Germans had thought of the French. The Tiger called the Germans: *Huns*, "a savage" brand of the nomads who

invaded Europe in the fourth century! He likened them to the nomads of Arabia and the barbarian Turks!
The Germans didn't like him either and believed themselves superior to his culture and local practices. After the war, his incessant business was to embarrass them. But how? The French army was full of Senegalese whom, on his orders, the French commanders placed on Germany's borders, like adding Insult to Injury.

> One of the most important problems connected with the limitation of armament, as it affects civilization, has attracted, since the Peace Conference, almost no attention. This concerns the right of the great nations of the world, which have in tutelage the weaker races of Africa and Asia, to arm these natives and use them as soldiers in fighting their own wars.

> There were those at Paris who were profoundly concerned over the growth of this ugly practice, who saw in use, in the great war, of hundreds of thousands of Chinese, Siamese, Senegalese, Arabs, and Sikhs, a profound menace to future civilization [...]

> The use by the French of colored troops in Germany after the war closed – which the Germans resented as the: "black horror of the Rhine" – caused great bitterness of feeling.

> Leaders who, like General Smuts of South Africa, knew most of the danger, were most concerned. He had had experience with what it might mean in the struggle to overcome the Germans in East Africa. [...]

> It was one of the accepted ideas of the German colonial enthusiasts that great native armies could

be built in German Africa, which could be used not only in African wars but for fighting for German causes elsewhere in the world.

Herr Zimmerman[78] anticipated that in fifty years, the German colonial empire would have a population of fifty million Blacks and half a million Whites. If properly trained, an army of one million natives could be mobilized at any time. [...][79]

That was a question which Mark Sykes and Georges Picot had tried to address in their roadmaps of dotted lines that they had drawn and modified, as the 'field battles required,' in 1915, throughout 1916, and which Clemenceau, himself, had had a cursory look and approved *post-mortem*.

Nevermind all the rattling, Mark Sykes and Georges Picot, the architects of the victories in the Levant, Arabia, and the Middle East, didn't anticipate that one day soon, beneath their upstanding military successes lay sharp and cheap political divisions.

From 1916, up until March 1922, during all these years, America, from beginning to end, had been met with obstruction, evasion, and equivocation on the part of France and England. America had been watching how the

---

[78] Arthur Zimmermann (1864 – 1940) was State Secretary for Foreign Affairs of the German Empire from 22 November 1916 until his resignation on August 6, 1917.

[79] Excerpts from Secret Minutes of Arguments of Big Four about "Shall Savage Races Be Armed?" The American Archives as laid down in report by Ray Stannard Baker and published by Special arrangement with the McClure Newspaper Syndicate. Also, refer to Clarion-Ledger – Mississippi, Sunday February 12, 1922 and a lot more newspapers published in 1922.

Italians had been grappling to take a more significant share than already allotted to them.

After the Russian Revolution and America's isolationism policy, whoever occupies a territory shall also impose their social system.
Everyone imposes his governance methods as far as his army is required to do so under the guise of Mandates and Protectorates.

Thus, Sykes-Picot was the last chapter, done by an excellent skill-combination of the military (Sykes) and political (Picot).
Their 'marriage of convenience' kept the Levant and the Middle East on their toes to the highest point and then let it fall.
The climax came when England and France made a break for the safety of their positions.
Also, another climax came when it was felt by French Nationalists, who formed the majority of the Chamber, that Sykes-Picot had been purely single, and would have the effect of placing France in the position of a protected and inferior nation.
The battles waged *within the dotted lines* did not altogether cause half as much description, nor were they preceded by half as many commentaries in the British and French media.
It is that individual sets of troops– aspirants to office or promotion – soldiers who live in the smiles of the Lieutenant or the General, have made of the roadmaps and the dotted lines of Sykes-Picot appear ridiculous.
It is also that Clemenceau's unpredictable, quick wits made of the military *'dotted lines'* appear absurd and puerile.

ANNEX I

Catalogue Reference: CAB/24/9 Image Reference:0071

Memorandum communicated by Sir M. Sykes, May 8, 1916.

M. GEORGES PICOT returned from Petrograd on Friday, the 5th, having concluded with the Russian Minister for Foreign Affairs the business committed to him by the French Government relative to the Arab question.

The following are the letters which were mutually exchanged between M. Paleologue and M. Sazonoff: —

(I.)
M, Sazonof, Ministre des Affaires Etrangères, a M. Paleologue, Ambassadeur *de France en Russie.*
Petrograd, le 26 avril, 1916.
M. l'Ambassadeur,
En me référant aux aide-memoire adressés par le Ministère Imperial des Affaires Etrangères à l'Ambassade de France en date du 4/17 et 8/21 mars, année courante, J'ai l'honneur de faire connaitre à votre Excellence qu'à la suite des entretiens que j'ai eus avec M. Georges Picot, délégué special du Gouvernement Français, relativement à la reconnaissance de l'accord qui serait établi entre la France et l'Angleterre pour la constitution d'un Etat ou d'une fédération d'Etats arabes et à l'attribution des Territoires de la Syrie, de la Cilicie et de la Mésopotamie, le Gouvernement Imperial est prêt à

sanctionner l'arrangement établi sur les bases qui lui ont été indiquées aux conditions suivantes:

1. La Russie annexerait les regions d'Erzeroum, de Trébizonde, de Van et de Bitlis, jusqu'à un point à determiner sur le littoral de la mer Noire à l'ouest de Trébizonde;

2. La region du Kurdistān située au sud de Van et de Bitlis entre Mouch, Sert, le cours du Tigre, Djeziret-ibn-Omar, la ligne de faîtes des montagnes qui dominent Amadia, et la region de Mergavar serait cédée à la Russie, qui, en revanche, reconnaitrait à la France la propriété du territoire compris entre l'Ala Dagh, Césarée, l'Ak Dagh, l'Yildiz Dagh, Zara, Eghin et Kharpout. En outre, à partir de la région de Mergavar, la frontière de l'Arabie suivrait la ligne de faîtes des montagnes qui limitent actuellement les territoires ottoman et persan. Ces limites sont indiquées d'une manière générale et sous reserve des modifications de détail à proposer par la Commission de Délimitation qui se réunira ultérieurement sur les lieux.

Le Gouvernement Imperial consent, en outre, à admettre que dans toutes les parties du territoire ottoman ainsi cédées à la Russie les concessions de chemins de fer et autres accordées à des Français par le Gouvernement ottoman seront maintenues.

Si le Gouvernement Imperial exprime le désir qu'elles soient modifiées ultérieurement en vue de les mettre en harmonie avec les lois de l'Empire, cette modification aura lieu d'accord avec le Gouvernement de la Republique.

En ce qui concerne les institutions, administrations, établissements religieux, scolaires, hospitaliers, &c, relevant des deux nations, ils continueraient à jouir des privilèges qui leur étaient accordés jusqu'ici par les traités, accords et contrats conclus avec le Gouvernement ottoman. Il demeure, toutefois, entendu qu'en stipulant une telle réserve les deux Gouvernements n'ont pas voulu exiger pour l'avenir le maintien des droits de juridiction, du protectorat religieux et des Capitulations dans les regions qui seraient ainsi annexées à la Russie et à la France, mais seulement assurer la survivance des institutions et établissements actuellement existant et ouvrir la voie, après la conclusion de la paix, à une négotiation entre les deux Puissances.

Enfin, les deux Gouvernements admettent en principe que chacun des Etats qui annexerait des territoires turcs devrait participer au service de la Dette ottomane.

Veuillez, &c.

SAZONOF.

(II)

M. Paleologue, Ambassadeur de France, en Russie, à M. Sazonof, Ministre des *Affaires Etrangères*.

Ambassade de France en Russie, Petrograd,

le 26 avril, 1916.

M. le Ministre,

J'ai l'honneur d'accuser réception de la communication que votre Excellence m'a adressée à la date de ce jour, relativement à la reconnaissance par le Gouvernement Imperial, aux conditions suivantes, de l'accord qui serait établi entre la France et l'Angleterre pour constituer un Etat ou une fédération des Etats arabes et assurer l'attribution des territoires de la Syrie, de la Cilicie et de la Mésopotamie sur les bases qui lui ont été indiquées par le délègué special du Gouvernement français. De son côté, le Gouvernement de la Republique m'a chargé de vous faire connaitre qu'il a décidé de sanctionner l'arrangement dont il s'agit:

1. La Russie annexerait les régions d'Erzeroum, de Trébizonde de Van et de Bitlis jusqu'à un point à déterminer sur le littoral de la mer Noire à l'ouest de Trébizonde;

2. La region du Kurdistān située au sud de Van et de Bitlis entre Mouch, Sert, le cours du Tigre, Djeziret-ibn-Omar, la ligne de faîtes des montagnes qui dominent Amadia et la région de Mergavar serait cédée à la Russie, qui, en revanche, attribuerait à la France les territoires

compris entre l'Ala Dagh, Césarée, l'Ak Dagh, L'Yildiz Dagh, Zara, Eghin et Kharpout. En outre, à partir de la région de Mergavar, la frontière de Arabie suivrait la ligne de faîtes des montagnes qui limitent actuellement les territoires ottoman et persan. Ces limites sont indiquées d'une manière générale et sous réserve des modifications de détail à proposer par la Commission de Delimitation qui se réunira ultérieurement sur les lieux.

Le Gouvernent de la Republique prend acte avec satisfaction de ce que le Gouvernement Imperial consent, en outre, à admettre que dans toutes les parties du territoire ottoman ainsi cédées à la Russie les concessions de chemins de fer et autres accordées à des Français par le Gouvernement ottoman seront maintenues. Si le Gouvernement Imperial exprime le désir qu'elles soient modifiées ultérieurement en vue de les mettre en harmonie avec les lois de l'Empire, cette modification aurait lieu d'accord avec le Gouvernement de la Republique.

En ce qui concerne les institutions, administrations, établissements religieux, scolaires hospitaliers, &c, relevant des deux nations, ils continueront à jouir des privilèges qui leur étaient accordés jusqu'ici par les traités, accords et contrats conclus avec le Gouvernement ottoman. Il demeure, toutefois, entendu qu'en stipulant une telle reserve les deux Gouvernements n'ont pas voulu exiger pour l'avenir le maintien des droits de juridiction, du protectorat religieux et des Capitulations dans les regions qui seraient ainsi annexées à la Russie et à la France, mais seulement assurer la survivance des institutions et établissements actuellement existant et ouvrir la voie, après la conclusion de la paix, à une négociation dont l'amitié des deux pays ne permet pas de mettre en doute l'heureuse solution.

Enfin, les deux Gouvernements admettent en principe que chacun des Etats qui annexerait des territoires turcs devrait participer au service de la Dette ottomane.

Veuillez, &c.

PALEOLOGUE.

[88317]
M. Gambon to Sir Edward Grey. — (Received May 10.)
Ambassade de France, Londres,
le 9 mai, 1916.
M. le Secrétaire d'Etat,
DESIREUX d'entrer dans les vues du Gouvernement, du Roi et de chercher à détacher les Arabes des Turcs en facilitant la création d'un Etat ou d'une confédération d'Etats arabes, le Gouvernement de la République avait accepté l'invitation qui lui avait été adressée par le Cabinet britannique en vue de fixer les limites de cet Etat et des regions syriennes où les intérêts français sont prédominants.

A la suite des conférences qui ont eu lieu à ce sujet à Londres et des pourparlers qui se sont poursuivis à Pétrograd un accord s'est établi. J'ai été chargé de faire connaitre à votre Excellence que le Gouvernement français accepte les limites telles quelles ont été fixées sur les cartes signées par Sir Mark Sykes et M. Georges Picot, ainsi que les conditions diverses formulées au cours de ces discussions.

II demeure donc entendu que:

1, La France et la Grande-Bretagne sont disposées à reconnaitre et à soutenir un Etat arabe indépendant ou une confédération d'Etats arabes dans les zones (A) et (B), indiquées sur la carte ci-jointe, sous la suzeraineté d'un chef arabe. Dans la zone (A) la France, et dans la zone (B). la Grande-Bretagne, auront un droit de priorité sur les entreprises et les emprunts locaux. Dans la zone (A) la France, et dans la zone (B) la Grande-Bretagne, seront seules à fournir des conseillers ou des fonctionnaires étrangers à la demande de l'Etat arabe ou de la confédération d'Etats arabes.

2. Dans la zone bleue la France, et dans la zone rouge la Grande-Bretagne, seront autorisées à établir telle

administration directe ou indirecte ou tel contrôle qu'elles désirent et quelle jugeront convenable d'établir après entente avec l'Etat ou la confédération d'Etats arabes.

3. Dans la zone jaune sera établie une administration internationale, dont la forme devra être décidée après consultation avec la Russie, et ensuite d'accord avec les autres Alliés et les représentants du Cherif de La Mecque.

4. Il sera accordé à la Grande-Bretagne : (1) les ports de Haïfa et d'Acre ; (2) la garantie d'une quantité définie d'eau du Tigre et de l'Euphrate dans la zone (A) pour la zone (B). Le Gouvernement de Sa Majesté, de son côté, s'engage à n'entreprendre à aucun moment des négociations en vue de la cession de Chypre à une tierce Puissance sans le consentement préalable du Gouvernement français.

5. Alexandrette sera un port franc en ce qui concerne le commerce de l'Empire britannique, et il ne sera pas établi de différence de traitement dans les droits de ports, ni d'avantages particuliers refusés à la marine ou aux marchandises anglaises; il y aura libre transit pour les marchandises anglaises par Alexandrette et par chemin de fer à travers la zone bleue, que ces marchandises soient destinées à la zone rouge, la zone (B), la zone (A), ou en proviennent; et aucune différence de traitement ne sera établie directement ou indirectement au dépens des marchandises anglaises sur quelque chemin de fer que ce soit comme au dépens de marchandises ou de navires anglais dans tout port desservant les zones mentionnées.

Caifa *(Haifa)* sera, un port franc en ce qui concerne le commerce de la France, de ses colonies et de ses protectorats, et il n'y aura ni différence de traitement ni avantage dans les droits de port qui puisse être refusé à la marine et aux marchandises françaises. Il y aura libre transit pour les marchandises françaises par Caifa *(Haifa)* et par le chemin de fer anglais à travers la zone jaune, que ces marchandises soient en provenance ou à destination de la zone bleue, de la zone (A) ou de la zone (B); et il n'y aura aucune différence de traitement directe ou indirecte au dépens des marchandises françaises sur quelque chemin de fer que ce soit comme au dépens des marchandises ou des navires français dans quelque port que ce soit desservant les zones mentionnées.

6. Dans la zone (A), le Chemin de Fer de Bagdad ne sera pas prolongé vers le sud au delà de Mossoul, et dans la zone (B) vers le nord au delà de Samarra, jusqu'à ce qu'un chemin de fer reliant Bagdad à Alep dans la vallée de l'Euphrate ait été terminé, et cela seulement avec le concours des deux Gouvernements.

7. La Grande-Bretagne aura le droit de construire, d'administrer et d'être seule Propriétaire d'un chemin de fer reliant Caifa avec la zone (B), et elle aura, en outre, un droit perpétuel de transporter ses troupes, en tout temps, le long de cette ligne. Il doit être entendu par les deux Gouvernements que ce chemin de fer doit faciliter la jonction de Bagdad et de Caifa, et il est, de plus, entendu que, si les difficultés techniques et les dépenses encourues pour l'entretien de cette ligne de jonction dans la zone jaune en rendent l'exécution impraticable, le Gouvernement français sera disposé à envisager que ladite ligne puisse traverser le polygone Barries-Keis Maril-Silbrad-Tel Hotsda-Mesuire avant d'atteindre la zone (B).

8. Pour une période de vingt ans les tarifs douaniers turcs resteront en vigueur dans toute l'étendue des zones bleue et rouge aussi bien que dans les zones (A) et (B), et aucune augmentation dans les taux des droits ou changement des droits *ad valorem* en droits spécifiques ne pourra être faite si ce n'est avec le consentement des *deux* Puissances.

Il n'y aura pas de douanes intérieures entre aucune des zones ci-dessus mentionnées. Les droits de douanes prélevables sur les marchandises destinées à l'intérieur seront exigés aux ports d'entrée et transmis à l'administration de la zone destinataire.

9. Il sera entendu que le Gouvernement français n'entreprendra, à aucun moment, aucune négociation pour

la cession de ses droits, et ne cèdera les droits qu'il possédera dans la zone bleue à aucune autre tierce Puissance, si ce n'est l'Etat ou la confédération d'Etats arabes, sans l'agrément préalable du Gouvernement de Sa Majesté, qui, de son côté, donnera une assurance semblable au Gouvernement français en ce qui concerne la zone rouge.

10. Les Gouvernements anglais et français se mettront d'accord pour ne pas acquérir, et ne consentiront pas qu'une tierce Puissance acquière, de possessions territoriales dans la péninsule arabique ou construise une base navale dans les îles sur la côte est de la mer Rouge. Ceci, toutefois, n'empêchera pas telle rectification de la frontière d'Aden qui pourra être jugée nécessaire, par suite de la récente agression des Turcs.

11. Les négociations avec les Arabes pour les frontières de l'Etat ou de la confédération d'Etats arabes continueront par les mêmes voies que précédemment aux noms des deux Puissances.

12. Il est entendu, en outre, que des mesures de contrôle pour l'importation des armes sur le territoire arabe seront envisagées par les deux Gouvernements.

Je serais obligé à votre Excellence, au cas où ces conditions auraient l'agrément du Gouvernement du Roi, de vouloir bien me le faire connaitre.

Veuillez, &c.

PAUL CAMBON

[87247]
Sir Edward Grey to M. Cambon.
(Secret.)
Foreign Office, May 15, 1916.
Your Excellency,
I SHALL have the honour to reply fully in a further note to your Excellences' note of the 9th instant, relative to the creation of an Arab State, but I should meanwhile be grateful if your Excellency could assure me that in those

regions which, under the conditions recorded in that communication, become entirely French, or in which French interests are recognised as predominant, any existing British concessions, rights of navigation or development, and the rights and privileges of any British religious, scholastic, or medical institutions will be maintained.

His Majesty's Government are, of course, ready to give a reciprocal assurance in regard to the British area.

I have, &c.

E. GREY.

[92559]

M. Cambon to Sir Edward Grey. — (Received May 16.)

Ambassade de France, Londres,

15 *mai,* 1916

M. le Secrétaire d'Etat,

PAR sa communication de ce jour votre Excellence m'a exprimé le désir, avant de répondre à ma lettre en date du 9 de ce mois relative à la création d'un Etat arabe, de recevoir l'assurance que dans les regions qui deviendront françaises ou dans celles où les intérêts français seraient prédominants, les concessions et droits de navigation, ainsi que les droits et privilèges de tous les établissements religieux, scolaires et médicaux britanniques, seraient maintenus. II serait entendu, par contre, que les mêmes droits seraient reconnus à la France par le Gouvernement du Roi dans la sphère dévolue a l'Angleterre.

J'ai l'honneur de faire connaître à votre Excellence que le Gouvernement français est prêt à sanctionner les diverses concessions britanniques ayant date certaine antérieure à la guerre dans les regions qui lui seraient attribuées ou qui relèveraient de son action. Quant aux établissements médicaux, scolaires ou religieux, ils continueraient' à fonctionner comme par le passé, étant entendu toutefois qu'une telle réserve ne comporte pas le maintien des droits de juridiction et des capitulations dans ces territoires.

Veuillez, &c.
PAUL CAMBON.

[87247]
Sir Edward Grey to M. Cambon.
(Secret.) ....
Foreign Office, May 16, 1916.
Your Excellency,

I HAVE the honour to acknowledge the receipt of your Excellency's note of the 9th instant, stating that the French Government accept the limits of a future Arab State, or Confederation of States, and of those parts of Syria where French interests predominate, together with certain conditions attached thereto, such as they result from recent discussions in London and Petrograd on the subject.

I have the honour to inform your Excellency in reply that the acceptance of the whole project, as it now stands, will involve the abdication of considerable British interests, but, since His Majesty's Government recognise the advantage to the general cause of the Allies entailed in producing a more favourable internal political situation in Turkey, they are ready to accept the arrangement now arrived at, provided that the co-operation of the Arabs is secured, and that the Arabs fulfil the conditions and obtain the towns of Homs, Hama, Damascus, and Aleppo.

It is accordingly understood between the French and British Governments—

1. That. France and Great Britain are prepared to recognise and uphold an independent Arab State or a Confederation of Arab States in the areas (a) and (6) marked on the annexed map, under the suzerainty of an Arab chief. That in area *(a)* France, and in area *(b)* Great Britain, shall have priority of right of enterprise and local loans. That in area (a) France, and in area (o) Great Britain, shall alone supply advisers or foreign

functionaries at the request of the Arab State or Confederation of Arab States.

2. That in the blue area France, and in the red area Great Britain, shall be allowed to establish such direct or indirect administration or control as they desire and as they may think fit to arrange with the Arab State or Confederation of Arab States.

3. That in the brown area there shall be established an international administration, the form of which is to be decided upon after consultation with Russia and subsequently in consultation with the other Allies, and the representatives of the Shereef of Mecca.

4. That Great Britain is accorded (1) the ports of Haifa and Acre, (2) guarantee of a given supply of water from the Tigris and Euphrates in area (a) for area (b).

His Majesty's Government, on their part, undertakes that they will at no time enter into negotiations for the cession of Cyprus to any third Power without the previous consent of the French Government.

5. That Alexandretta shall be a free port as regards the trade of the British Empire, and that there shall be no discrimination in port charges or facilities as regards British shipping and British goods; that there shall be freedom of transit for British goods through Alexandretta and by railway through the blue area, whether those goods are intended for or originate in the red area, or (b) area, or area (a); and there shall be no discrimination, direct or indirect, against British goods on any railway or against British goods or ships at any port serving the areas mentioned.

That Haifa shall be a free port as regards the trade of France, her dominions, and protectorates, and there shall be no discrimination in port charges or facilities as regards French shipping and French goods. There shall be freedom of transit for French goods through Haifa and by the British railway through the brown area, whether those goods are intended for or originate in the blue area, area (a), or area (b), and there shall be no discrimination, direct or indirect, against French goods on any railway, or against French goods or ships at any port serving the areas mentioned.

6. That in area (a) the Bagdad Railway shall not be extended southwards beyond Mosul, and in area (b) northwards beyond Samarra, until a railway connecting Bagdad with Aleppo via the Euphrates Valley has been completed, and then only with the concurrence of the two Governments.

7. That Great Britain has the right to build, administer, and be the sole owner of a railway connecting Haifa with area (b), and shall have a perpetual right to transport troops along such a line at all times.

It is to be understood by both Governments that this railway is to facilitate the connection of Bagdad with Haifa by rail, and it is further understood that, if the engineering difficulties and expense entailed by keeping this connecting line in the brown area only make the project unfeasible, that the French Government shall be prepared to consider that the line in question may also traverse the polygon Banias-Keis Marib-Salkhad Tell Otsda-Mesmie before reaching area (b).

8. For a period of twenty years the existing Turkish customs tariff shall remain in force throughout the whole of the blue and red areas, as well as in areas (a) and (b), and no increase in the rates of duty or conversion from *ad valorem* to specific rates shall be made except by agreement between the two Powers.

There shall be no interior customs barriers between any of the above-mentioned areas. The customs duties leviable on goods destined for the interior shall be collected at the port of entry and handed over to the administration of the area of destination.

9. It shall be agreed that the French Government will at no time enter into any negotiations for the cession of their rights and will not cede such rights in the blue area to any third Power, except the Arab State or Confederation of Arab States, without the previous agreement of His

Majesty's Government, who, on their part, will give a similar undertaking to the French Government regarding the red area.

10. The British and French Governments shall agree that they will not themselves acquire and will not consent to a third Power acquiring territorial possessions in the Arabian Peninsula, nor consent to a third Power constructing a naval base on the islands of the east coast of the Red Sea. This, however, shall not prevent such adjustment of the Aden frontier as may be necessary in consequence of recent Turkish aggression.

11. The negotiations with the Arabs as to the boundaries of the Arab State or Confederation of Arab States shall be continued through the same channel as heretofore on behalf of the two Powers.

12. It is agreed that measures to control the importation of arms into the Arab territories will be considered by the two Governments.

I have further the honour to state that, in order to make the agreement complete, His Majesty's Government are proposing to the Russian Government to exchange notes analogous to those exchanged by the latter and your Excellency's Government on 26th April last. Copies of these notes will be communicated to your Excellency as soon as exchanged.

I would also venture to remind your Excellency that the conclusion of the present agreement raises, for practical consideration, the question of the claims of Italy to a share in any partition or rearrangement of Turkey in Asia, as formulated in article 9 of the agreement of 26th April 1915, between Italy and the Allies.

His Majesty's Government further considers that the Japanese Government should be informed of the arrangements now concluded.

I have, &c.

E. GREY.

[93696]
Sir Edward Grey to Count Bencliendorff.
(Secret.)
Foreign Office, May 23, 1916.
Your Excellency,

I HAVE received, from the French Ambassador in London copies of the notes exchanged between the Russian and French Governments on the 26th ultimo, by which your Excellency's Government recognise, subject to certain conditions, the arrangement made between Great Britain and France, relative to the constitution of an Arab State or a Confederation of Arab States, and to the partition of the territories of Syria, Cilicia, and Mesopotamia, provided that the co-operation of the Arabs is secured.

His Majesty's Government take act with satisfaction that your Excellency's Government concur with the limits set forth in that arrangement, and I have now the honour to inform your Excellency that His Majesty's Government, on their part, in order to make the arrangement complete, are also prepared to recognise the conditions formulated by the Russian Government and accepted by the French Government in the notes exchanged at Petrograd on the 26th ultimo.

In so far, then, as these arrangements directly affect the relations between Russia and Great Britain, I have the honour to invite the acquiescence of your Excellency's Government in agreement on the following terms: —

1. That Russia shall annex the regions of Erzeroum, Trebizond, Van. and Bitlis, up to a point subsequently to be determined on the littoral of the Black Sea to the west of Trebizond.

2. That the region of Kurdistan to the south of Van and of Bitlis between Mush, Sert, the course of the Tigris, Jezireh-ben-Omar, the crest-line of the mountains which dominate Amadia, and the region of Merga Var, shall be ceded to Russia; and that starting from the region of Merga Var, the frontier of the Arab State shall follow the

166

crest-line of the mountains which at present divide the Ottoman and Persian Dominions. These boundaries are indicated in a general manner and are subject to modifications of detail to be proposed later by the Delimitation Commission which shall meet on the spot.

3. That the Russian Government undertakes that, in all parts of the Ottoman territories thus ceded to Russia, any concessions accorded to British subjects by the Ottoman Government shall be maintained. If the Russian Government express the desire that such concessions should later be modified in order to bring them, into harmony with the laws of the Russian Empire, this modification shall only take place in agreement with the British Government.

4. That in all parts of the Ottoman territories thus ceded to Russia, existing British rights of navigation and development, and the rights and privileges of any British religious, scholastic, or medical institutions shall be maintained. His Majesty's Government, on their part, undertakes that similar Russian rights and privileges shall be maintained in those regions which, under the conditions of this agreement, become entirely British, or in which British interests are recognised as predominant.

5. The two Governments admit in principle that every State which annexes any part of the Ottoman Empire is called upon to participate in the service of the Ottoman Debt.

I have, &c,

E. GREY.

[168743]

M. Cambon to Viscount Grey. — (Received August 26.)

Ambassade de France, Londres,

le 25 aout, 1916.

M. le Vicomte,

LES termes "protégé un Etat arabe indépendant" et "protect an independent Arab State" employés dans les lettres que nous avons échangées, les 9 et 16 mai dernier, relativement à la question de Syrie, ayant semblé a votre Seigneurie devoir prêter à des erreurs interprétation, en pouvant laisser croire qu'il s'agit d'une sorte de protectorat, alors que nous avons seulement entendu garantir la pleine indépendance du nouvel Etat, je ne vois, en ce qui me concerne, aucun inconvenient à modifier ces expressions, suivant le désir que vous m'en avez exprimé.

Il me semble que les mots "soutenir" et "uphold" rendraient plus exactement notre pensée. Si votre Seigneurie partage ce sentiment, la substitution pourrait en être faite dans les documents originaux.

Veuillez, &c.

PAUL CAMBON.

[168743]

The Marquess of Crewe to M. Cambon.

Foreign Office, August 30, 1916.

Your Excellency,

I HAVE the honour to acknowledge the receipt of your Excellency's note of the 25th instant, suggesting that for the words "protect" (protéger) an independent Arab State," which occur in the notes exchanged on the 9th and 16th last, on the subject of Asiatic Turkey, the words "uphold (soutenir) an independent Arab State" should be read.

In reply, I have the honour to state that I see no objection to the adoption of the word suggested by your Excellency, and I have accordingly caused the necessary alteration to be made in the original text of your note of the 9th May.

I have, &c.

CREWE.

[180511]

Count Benckendorff to Viscount Grey. — (Received September 1.)

Ambassade Impériale de Russie, Londres,
le 1er septembre, 1916.

M. le Vicomte,

PAR une note en date du 23 mai, année courante, votre Seigneurie a bien voulu m'informer qu'elle avait reçu de l'Ambassadeur de France à Londres une copie des notes échangées, le 26 avril, année courante, entre les Gouvernements français et russe, par lesquelles le Gouvernement Imperial accepte, à certaines conditions, l'arrangement conclu entre la Grande-Bretagne et la France relativement à la création d'un Etat ou d'une confédération d'Etats arabes, ainsi qu'au partage des territoires de la Syrie, la Cilicie et la Mésopotamie, pourvu que la coopération des Arabes soit assurée.

En outre, votre Seigneurie a bien voulu ajouter que le Gouvernement Royal est disposé, en vue de rendre l'arrangement complet, à reconnaitre les conditions formulées par le Gouvernement Imperial et acceptées par le Gouvernement français dans les notes échangées à Pétrograd le 26 avril, 1916.

J'ai, en conséquence, l'honneur de porter à la connaissance de votre Seigneurie que le Gouvernement de Sa Majesté britannique et le Gouvernement Impérial sont tombés d'accord sur les points suivants :

1. La Russie annexera les regions d'Erzeroum, Trebizond, Van et Bitlis jusqu'a un point sur le littoral de la mer Noire a l'ouest de Trebizond à déterminer ultérieurement.

2. La region du Kurdistan au sud de Van et Bitlis comprise entre Much, Sert, lecours du Tigre, Jezireh-ben-Omar, la ligne des montagnes dominant Amadia et la region de Merga Var, sera cédée a la Russie. A partir de la région de Merga Var, la frontière de l'Etat arabe suivra la ligne des montagnes divisant actuellement les territoires ottomans et persans. Les frontières susmentionnées sont indiquées d'une manière générale et sont sujettes à des modifications de detail devant être proposées ultérieurement par la Commission de Délimitation qui se réunira sur les lieux.

3. Le Gouvernement Impérial consent de maintenir dans toutes les parties du territoire ottoman ainsi cédées à la Russie toutes concessions accordées par le Gouvernement ottoman aux sujets britanniques. Dans le cas où le Gouvernement Imperial exprimerait le désir que ces concessions soient modifiées ultérieurement dans le but de les faire concorder avec les exigences des lois russes, cette modification aura lieu d'accord avec le Gouvernement britannique.

4. Dans toutes les parties des territoires ottomans ainsi cédées à la Russie, les droits existants de navigation et les concessions diverses consenties au Gouvernement britannique, ainsi que les droits et privilèges des institutions religieuses, scolaires et médicales britanniques, devront être maintenus. Le Gouvernement de Sa Majesté britannique reconnait, de son côté, que les droits et privilèges similaires reconnus à la Russie dans les territoires attribués en toute souveraineté à la Grande-Bretagne où dans lesquels les intérêts britanniques sont reconnus comme prédominants par le présent, arrangement devront être maintenus.

Toutefois, je suis chargé de formuler la réserve suivante : Les avantages consentis par cet article, affectant la legislation de l'Empire en matière de cabotage, législation qui a déjà donne lieu à des reserves spéciales dans plusieurs traités internationaux conclus entre la Russie et diverses autres Puissances, cette question ne saurait, dans l'opinion du Gouvernement Imperial, être préjugée dès maintenant, mais elle pourra être soumise ultérieurement à l'amical examen des deux Puissances en vue d'arriver à une solution satisfaisante pour l'une et pour l'autre.

5. Les deux Gouvernements admettent le principe que chaque Etat annexant une partie quelconque de l'Empire ottoman sera tenu de participer au service de la dette ottomane.

Cest avec la plus haute consideration, &c.

BENCXENDORFF.

[207447]
Viscount Grey to Count Benckendorff.
Foreign Office, October 23, 1916.
Your Excellency,

IN reply to your Excellency's note of the 1st ultimo, regarding the arrangement between Great Britain, Russia, and France, relative to the creation of an Arab State, or of a confederation of Arab States, and to the partition of the territories of Syria, Cilicia, and Mesopotamia, provided that the co-operation of the Arabs is secured, I have the honour to state that His Majesty's Government take note of the reservation formulated by the Imperial Russian Government at the end of article 4 of the arrangement respecting the rights of the Imperial Government to *grand cabotage* in the Black Sea, and of the desire manifested by that Government that this question should be submitted later to a friendly examination by the Governments of the parties interested.

I have, &c. GREY OF FALLODON.

ANNEX II

Catalogue Reference: CAB/24/95 Image Reference: 0037
[This Document is the Property of His Britannic Majesty's Government.]
Printed for the Cabinet. December 1919.
CONFIDENTIAL

THIS is the memorandum (on the lines of that upon the Baltic States) which the Cabinet asked me a little while ago to have prepared in the Foreign Office on the subject of the Transcaucasian Republics and situation.

C. OF K.

December 24, 1919.

TRANSCAUCASIA.

The component parts of Transcaucasia were incorporated in the Russian Empire at various dates. The whole of this country only finally came under Russian rule in 1878, when, under the terms of the Treaty of Berlin, Turkey ceded the provinces of Batoum, Olti, and Ardahan to Russia.

The people inhabiting this country are Moslems (both Shiahs and Sunnis), Christians (Orthodox Greek and Russian, Armenians, Lutherans), and Jews. There are supposed to be eighteen distinct races and forty-eight different dialects.

The area is at present divided into four districts:— Georgia, the Armenian Republic of Erivan, the Azerbaijan Republic and the Batoum province. In the notes which follow, however, it has been necessary to take account also of the province of Daghestan which, though lying to the north of the main Caucasus range, was included in the old Russian administrative area, and is a prominent factor in the present situation.

The population of Transcaucasia was estimated in 1915 at about 7,000,000,

composed of—

1,650,000 Georgians.

1,200,000 Armenians.

2,000,000 Moslems (Tartars and tribesmen).

  700,000 Daghestan hill tribes.

  325,000 Russians.

1,200,000 European colonists, foreigners, Jews, &c.

The natural resources of Transcaucasia have, under Russian influence, remained practically undeveloped, with the exception of the oilfields round Baku, the manganese deposits in Georgia and the large copper deposits in the Batoum province. Lack of communications and the restrictions placed by the former Russian Government on foreign capital probably account for this state of affairs. In and around the main Caucasus range are to be found copper, oil, lead, iron, coal and other minerals, together with an immense wealth of timber. An important fishing industry flourishes on. the shores of the Caspian, where also are to be found large supplies of Glauber salts.

In the development of waterpower also the country is rich in potentialities, as yet practically unexploited.

Position before the Russian Revolution of 1917.

Previous to the revolution Transcaucasia was administered as an integral part of the Russian Empire under a Viceroy whose seat was at Tiflis. The country was divided into six Government departments, *i.e.,* Black Sea provinces, Kutais, Tiflis, Baku, Erivan, Elizavetpol, and the then provinces of Batoum, Kars, and Daghestan.

Development since the Revolution.

In 1917, when the Russian Army left the Caucasian front with the cry of "Peace without annexation and indemnities!" and thus exposed the whole country to the attack of the Turks, a Transcaucasian Diet was formed at Tiflis in the shape of a coalition of Georgians, Tartars, and Armenians, with a view to the creation of a Federated Caucasus, and to the defence of the frontiers against Turkish invasion. This attempt at combination proved abortive. The Tartars of Azerbaijan were in open sympathy with the Turks, while the Armenians considered that the Georgians were attempting to establish a central Georgian Administration to govern the Caucasus from Tiflis.

Subsequently, at various dates and under different auspices the three districts known as Azerbaijan, Georgia, and Armenia established their own Governments and declared themselves independent republics. Although these republics are not formally recognised by His Majesty's Government, a certain *de facto* recognition is implied in the despatch to Tiflis last summer of Mr. Oliver Wardrop as chief British Commissioner in Transcaucasia. The measure of local recognition necessarily accorded by our military representatives during the period of British occupation is referred to below.

Short Historical Sketch of the several Areas,

(a.) Batoum Province.

The Batoum province would seem to have belonged to the old Kingdom of Georgia as early as the 7th century. In the 15th century, the Georgians lost it to the Turks, who eventually ceded it to the Russians in 1878.

The province was again ceded to Turkey in 1917 by the Brest-Litovsk Treaty. The Georgian National Assembly, not recognising this treaty, declared war on Turkey, but were unable to prevent her from overrunning the province, which remained in Turkish hands until the British occupied it in accordance with Clause 15 of the Turkish Armistice Terms, an occupation which is still in force.

(b.) Georgia.

The origin of the ancient Kingdom of Georgia belongs to the pre-Christian era.

In the Middle Ages - to go no further back - she played a prominent part in the later Crusades. Her history for several centuries thereafter is a long and chequered story of struggle with Turks and Persians. On the expansion of Russia towards the south, Georgia offered to unite with her northern neighbour to free the Caucasus from Turkish rule. In 1783, she concluded a treaty with Catherine II of Russia pledging her support to Russia in return for her complete internal independence. However, in 1801 Russia annexed Georgia, promising to maintain her previous rights and privileges in their entirety. This promise Russia never fulfilled, and the Georgians made the grievances arising from this breach of faith the subject of a fruitless petition addressed to The Hague Conference in 1907.

The Transcaucasian Diet, formed after the Russian Revolution, continued a chequered existence until June 1918. During this period, the British Military Mission at Tiflis, under the late Lieutenant-Colonel Pike, endeavoured to give it all the moral support possible, and financed it with a loan of 4,000,000 roubles in the hope that under the predominating influence of the Georgian statesmen, Jordani and Gegechkori, both members of the former Russian Duma, the Diet would be maintained and would continue the war on the side of the Allies.

Owing to the conflicting interests of the various races and to Bolshevism in the Georgian army, this policy failed. The establishment of a separate Georgian Parliament and a declaration of Georgian independence was the eventual outcome.

The trend of Georgian domestic policy since that date is dealt with below in its relation to Bolshevism. It will suffice to note here that recent reports testify to the remarkable growth of local government in Georgia. The Zemstva, established under the old Russian Government, have come to play a far more prominent part in the life of the country than was ever the case under the old regime. They have wide local powers and are shortly to send their own' elected representative to the Central Parliament at Tiflis.

According to Russian statistics (which include the province of Batoum), the country has an area of 13,456 square miles and a population of 2,512,000, including—

1,530,000 Georgians (Christian and Moslem).
  260,000 Armenians.
  129,000 Russians.
  213,000 Turki-speaking Moslems.
  126,000 Moslem tribesmen.

(c.) The Armenian Republic of Erivan.

The Armenian provinces of Erivan and Nakhichevan were ceded to Russia by Persia in accordance with the Treaty of Turkmanchai in 1828, while the rest of - Caucasian Armenia came definitely under Russian rule in 1878 when the provinces of Kars, Olti, and Ardahan were ceded to Russia by Turkey under the Treaty of Berlin.

The future of the Caucasian Armenians must inevitably be bound up with that of the Turkish Armenians, hundreds of thousands of whom are at present refugees in Transcaucasia. The Caucasian Armenians, while not so cultured as the Georgians, are thrifty and industrious. But the politics of the Erivan Republic are dominated by the notorious Armenian secret society known as "Dashnaktsutiun," which, with its programme of revenge and agitation, has recently manifested anti-British tendencies.

This Society is violently socialistic and revolutionary in origin, but its present policy in the Caucasus is centered on:

1. The acquisition of territory for the Erivan Republic.

2. The extension and equipment of the Armenian armed forces, and,

3. The propagation of the doctrine of the Dashnaks.

It seems improbable that sound democratic Government will be attained in the Erivan Republic until the activities of this Society have been ended. The Society by its methods of terrorism prevents the better and broader-minded elements of Armenian Society from taking up official positions. M. Khatissian, the Prime Minister, though himself at one time a Dashnak, has often been in conflict with the advanced members of the Society, while M. Papandjanian, a former member of the Russian Duma, and a representative of Armenia at the Peace Conference, is recently reported to have retired owing to differences of opinion with the Society.

According to Russian statistics, the population of the districts composing the present Republic of Erivan was estimated in 1912 at 1,081,000, of whom just under 600,000 were Armenians and the rest Moslems. In addition, there were, some 700,000 Armenians scattered up and down the rest of Transcaucasia, there being 230,000 in Georgia, 180,000 in Azerbaijan, and between 200,000 and 300,000 in the province of Batoum and the areas disputed between the respective Republics (see map).

In addition to the native population, it is estimated that there are in the Erivan Republic at present about 300,000 refugees from Turkish Armenia and some 30,000 Assyrians.

Throughout Transcaucasia, there is no more pressing problem than that of relief.

177

But at the present time, the Armenian Republic is economically in a probably worse state than any country in the world. The town and villages are full of refugees; the country has been devastated by the Turks. Food is hard to get, and in spite of the efforts of the American Relief Commission, there is much sickness and starvation, while, until at least quite recently, there has been continual fighting between Armenian and Moslem in the districts disputed with Azerbaijan.

(d.) The Azerbaijan Republic.

This province was ceded to Russia by Persia under the Treaty of Gulistan in 1813. Unlike Georgia, it has had no previous history as an independent State.

Before the advent of Russia, the country was alternately under the Georgian, Turkish and Persian rule. The inhabitants are a Persian type of Shiah Moslem, and their language is a Turkish dialect.

The territorial area of the present Republic is about 32,500 square miles, with a population of about 2,000,000, of whom 60 percent, are Mahommedans, 20 percent - Armenians, 6 percent. Russians, the remainder being Persians, Jews, &c. (Russian statistics).

The Apsheron Peninsula, on which the town of Baku is situated, is, in the eyes of the Russians at least, probably the most important district in all Transcaucasia.

Large oil deposits in this district produced in normal times the greater part of the oil fuel consumed in Russia. The port of Baku affords an easy means of communication with Astrakhan and, by way of the Volga, with all the main waterways of Russia, thus giving cheap and easy transport for the oil to the various markets. The town itself is a large supply center and a depot which feeds the Caucasus, Transcaspia, and North Persia with Russian supplies and foreign imports of all kinds. Although situated on an inland sea, Baku is the largest shipping center in the former Russian Empire. It has a fine natural harbour with adequate docks and repair yards.

In former times the shipping was mostly built on the Clyde and floated down the canals to the Volga on pontoons, and thence to Baku. However, of late years a certain amount of construction has been carried on in Baku itself. Apart from its oil, Baku has also important flour and cotton mills, the latter being fed by raw cotton from Transcaspia.

The Prime Minister who formed the first Cabinet was Khan Khoisky, a highly educated and extremely competent lawyer. He, however, subsequently gave place to M. Ussubekoff, an educated Tartar, of somewhat broader principles. It is reported that M. Ussubekoff is forming a new Cabinet, on which it is hoped Khan Khoisky will find a place as Minister for Foreign Affairs.

A Cabinet of which M. Ussubekolf, Khan Khoisky, and General Mechmandaroff are members would be in a strong position, and likely to take a liberal outlook on the Armenian question.

As a whole, the Azerbaijan Government may be considered more conservative than socialist. The wealthy merchant class is standing outside the actual Government, as it considers its influence more powerful when used indirectly.

(e.) Daghestan.

This province, formerly under the native khans, and lying to the north of the main Caucasus range, was also ceded by Persia to the Russians under the Treaty of Gulistan in 1813. It is a mountainous country peopled by wild hill tribes of various origin. After the Russian Revolution, it formed itself into the so-called "North Caucasus Republic," which sent delegates to the Peace Conference. Like Azerbaijan, the province has never been an independent State, and its people seem even less fit for self-determination. His Majesty's Government has therefore acquiesced in the occupation of the province by Denikm. The present position seems to be that a large part of the population has accepted the return to Russian rule, while another part is opposing the Volunteer Army by force and demanding independence or union with Azerbaijan.

Petrovsk is the Caspian port of Daghestan. As a port, it is inferior to Baku, but it has grown considerably in importance with the expansion of the Grozny oil fields (which are themselves situated in the Terek Cossack province).

Character and Aims of Georgia, Armenia, and Azerbaijan,

(a.) Common Factors.
All three Republics have three factors in common: —
1. Their genuine desire for independence.
2. Their desire to combat Bolshevism of the Soviet variety (as distinct from Socialistic principles of Government, which are accepted, notably by Georgia).
3. Their fear of Denikin and his policy of a United Russia (this is true in a less degree of the Armenians, who regard their reincorporation in Russia as precluded by the declarations made by the Allies during the war).

(b.) Internal Situation of the Republics.
With the exception of Georgia, the Republics suffer considerably from the lack of experienced administrators. This want adds greatly to the difficulties of the situation in Azerbaijan and Armenia, both of which have been devastated by the war to an extent which renders reconstruction of any kind the first necessity of the moment.

There are, nevertheless, hopeful signs. In Azerbaijan, the town of Baku is reported to be extremely well administered. The streets are well kept, there is an efficient police force, and the tramway service has recently been restarted. An army of about 30,000 men has been created in spite of difficulties arising from the fact that the Tartars under the old Russian regime were exempt from military service.

In Armenia, M. Khatissian, the Prime Minister, is a broad-minded and honest statesman, who has sacrificed his important business interests in Georgia in order to devote himself to the service of his native country.

The general internal situation of Armenia owing—

(a.) To the lack of competent administrators, and

(b.) To the difficult food situation and the large influx of refugees, can only be described as deplorable.

Of the three republics, Georgia is in much the best position. Her territory has escaped the ravages of war, while her people, who prided themselves, even under the old Russian regime, on the European origin of their civilisation, have the advantage over their neighbours in ability and culture. The internal order appears to be well maintained, and the sporadic outburst of Bolshevism which recurs at intervals are put down without difficulty and with commendable firmness. Of late the Georgian Government has complained of the All-Russian propaganda carried on in this territory by Denikin's agents and sympathisers sheltering themselves under the British military administration in the province of Batoum.

The economic situation of all the republics is very similar, their currency for purposes of foreign trade had depreciated to a point where it is practically valueless, the latest quotation being 7,800 roubles to the pound sterling. There are practically no imports, and the whole country is suffering from a dearth of manufactured goods, especially agricultural machinery.

The existing railways are marked on the accompanying map. The Batoum-Baku railway runs through the Batoum province, Georgia, and Azerbaijan, while the Batoum, Tiflis, Erivan-Djulfa line passes through Georgia, Armenia, Azerbaijan. A certain amount of rolling stock and engines was left after the evacuation of the Russian army in 1918, but there is a very considerable shortage in this respect. Owing to the lack of material and skilled

181

labour few repairs have been carried out. During the evacuation of the Turkish army after the Armistice, most of the existing rolling stock naturally, accumulated at the points where the Turkish troops left the country, notably Batoum and Kars. This led to great trouble, each of the Republics refusing to allow rolling stock and engines to leave its territory. A British railway control was finally established and through traffic provided for. Since the British evacuation, the three republics have by mutual consent continued on the lines set up by the British organisation. But railway control is still a fruitful source of friction, in particular between the Georgians and the British authorities at Batoum, who have, perforce, to use a Russian staff for the administration of the line in that province.

A new line was begun by the Russians connecting the Batoum-Baku line at Aliat with the railhead at Djulfa. The Azerbaijan Republic is now offering this work as a concession, and it is even reported to have been definitely acquired by the Italians.

(c.) Relations one with the other.

Azerbaijan and Georgia.
These two States have recently formed a defensive alliance against attack by Denikin, which also provides for arbitration of territorial disputes between themselves (see map).

Before this agreement, there had been considerable friction between the republics, due chiefly to the traditional hostility of the Georgians towards the Turks, under whose auspices the present Azerbaijan Republic was founded.

Georgia and Armenia.
In January 1919 Armenia and Georgia were drawn by Turkish intrigue (Denikm supporting Armenia) into war over the disputed territory of Borchalinsk. Peace was

arranged by the British Command at Tiflis and the disputed province declared to be a neutral zone. Much of the recent friction between the Armenians and the Georgians is due to the friendly attitude of the Armenian " Dashnaktsutiun " to General Denikin.

Thanks, however, in large part to the efforts of the British Chief Commissioner in Transcaucasia relations have considerably improved of late, and an agreement has now been signed providing for the transit of goods free of customs duty between the two countries. This agreement has already resulted in some alleviation of the food situation in Armenia.

Armenia and Azerbaijan.

The strained relations existing between these two republics date back to the Armenian massacres of 1905 in Baku and elsewhere in the Caucasus. The feelings engendered by these massacres were further stimulated during the war by the massacres and deportations of Armenians in Turkey and, on the other side, by massacres of Moslems instigated by the "Dashnaktsutiun" in Baku in March 1918 and in Caucasian Armenia in March, April, and May of the same year. Recent fighting has centered round the disputed territories of Nakhichevan, Zangazeur, Karabakh, and Sharur Daralageuz (see map).

After an unsuccessful attempt on the part of Colonel Haskell, sent out by the Peace Conference as Allied High Commissioner for Armenia, to settle the quarrel by the creation of Nachickhevan as a neutral zone, it is reported in the last few days that an agreement has been reached to settle territorial disputes by arrangement or to refer them to arbitration pending a decision by the Peace Conference or the Allies. The credit for this result must be shared by Mr. Wardrop and by Colonel Rhea (acting for Colonel Haskell during the latter's absence in Paris), but an early solution of the Transcaucasian question would seem to offer the only effective guarantee against a recrudescence of strife.

(d.) The position of the Republics vis-a-vis Denikin.

The absolute incompatibility of Denikin's aim of a reunited Russia with the aspirations of the republics for independence has already been noted.

The present military position between the two parties has been determined by the following arrangements: —

1. *On land.* — Early last summer, while the British troops were still in occupation of Transcaucasia, it was thought necessary to draw a dividing line between the spheres of Denikin and his Volunteer Army and that of the republics. This line follows in the main the central Caucasus range. But at its eastern and western extremities it has twice been subsequently modified (see map), partly at least under the pressure of events, especially in the case of Daghestan, where the whole province is now occupied by Denikin, and where His Majesty's Government have not felt called upon to embark on a serious dispute with him on behalf of a people whose character holds out no prospect of the creation on a stable basis of an independent State. The opposition which Denikin has been experiencing from part of the Daghestan population is freely attributed by him, not altogether without justification, to the intrigues of Georgia and Azerbaijan, and the situation in Daghestan is, therefore, a potential danger to the whole peace of the Caucasus.

On the west, the dividing line was finally fixed on the River Bzyb, but the Georgians still maintain forces at Gagri on the ground that the Bzyb River is an indefensible front. This question is a lively source of friction, and Denikin has recently refused to receive a Georgian deputation until the withdrawal to the Bzyb has taken place.

2. *On sea.* — As a necessary preliminary to the withdrawal of the British troops from Transcaucasia (with the exception of Batoum) which took place last August, the British naval flotilla in the Caspian, composed almost entirely of former Russian vessels, was handed over to

General Denikin on the express stipulation that he should not attempt to force his way into the port of Baku. While he has so far observed this stipulation, he has invoked the Russo-Persian Treaty of Turkmanchai to prevent the Azerbaijan flag being shown in the Caspian either on the merchant or war vessels.

In the Black Sea, the presence of a British naval force acted as a deterrent to Denikin's war vessels until the Georgians definitely refused to withdraw their forces on the Black Sea littoral to the south of the River Bzyb. Denikin then seized a Georgian guardship off Gagri which, at our request, had been previously disarmed, and one of his warships exchanged several shots with the Georgian guardship at Poti. Against this action, the Georgians have entered an official protest.

The hardly latent hostility between Denikin and the republics, with the ever-present danger of an explosion, is the key to the whole Transcaucasian position at the present time. Denikin has lately been reported to consider himself in a state of war with Georgia, and at the time of writing is also said to contemplate an attack on Baku, tempted by the prospect of controlling the oil supply there. He has recently brought economic weapons to bear—e.g.; he has imposed strict export restrictions against the republics in the area under his control—while the Georgians complain that his representatives at Batoum are carrying on All-Russia propaganda in that province, and are doing their best to discredit and depreciate the Georgian currency.

(e.) The Republics and Bolshevism.

Azerbaijan may be regarded as anti-Bolshevik, owing to the influence of the large Tartar landowners or khans and to the' presence of a wealthy commercial community.

But there is a large Russian working population in Baku which is distinctly Bolshevik in tendency and is supported by the Moslem society known as "Gumet," which is also supposed to be in close touch with the Committee of Union and Progress.

The Armenians in the Caucasus were regarded by the former Russian Government since 1905 as constituting the extreme revolutionary element in that region.

The Dashnaktsutiun is of extreme Socialist tendency but has in the past identified itself impartially with Bolshevism or reaction, in accordance with its own interests.

The pernicious influence of this society has already been commented upon, but the vagaries of Armenian politics can only be fairly appreciated if it is remembered that the Armenians in the Caucasus are surrounded on all sides by hostile peoples and that the experience of history has taught them to regard self-preservation as the one essential tenet of political faith.

The accusation of Bolshevik tendencies is so freely brought against Georgia that it is perhaps worthwhile pausing to examine how far it may be regarded as well-founded. During the last decade, the middle and lower classes in Georgia have shown very distinct socialistic and revolutionary tendencies. Two of the leaders of the Russian revolution under Kerensky were Georgians— Cheidze and Tseretelli. The probable reason for the attitude of the Georgian people was Russian oppression in which the Russianised Georgian aristocracy took a leading part.

At the time of the Bolshevik *coup d'état,* the country was riddled with extreme socialism, and the Bolsheviks looked like getting the upper hand. The Georgian Premier, M. Jordani, a democrat, but by no means a socialist, realised that he had no material force other than two regiments of Georgian cavalry, led by reactionary Georgian officers, with which to fight this internal movement; while on the other hand, owing to the desertion of the front by the Russian armies, Georgia was exposed to invasion by the Turk. In pursuance of the old

Russian policy of employing troops at a distance from their homes, the Georgian soldiers were on the northwest front in Russia, and it was known that they were deserting and returning to Georgia with their arms. They were saturated with Bolshevist doctrines, and the position seemed hopeless.

M. Jordani therefore invited the Socialists to join his Government, declared the Socialist Republic, nationalised all the land, and promised to nationalise all industry.

The Georgian army refused to continue the war, and the Georgian Government then accepted Germany's offer of (1) financial assistance; (2) a brigade to maintain internal order; (3) a guarantee that Germany's ally, Turkey, would under no circumstances cross the frontiers of Georgia. In fairness to the Georgians and M. Jordani, it must be remembered that a request for assistance in money and troops was first addressed to the British Military Mission, then at Tiflis, who gave some financial assistance, but were unable at that time to provide troops or accord recognition. From that date (May-June 1918) the whole of the energies of the Georgian Government led by Jordani and Gegechkori have been centered on reconstruction on social-democratic principles, and on the expulsion of the Bolshevik elements. Out of the chaos has evolved civilised government; private ownership is permitted up to a limit, the order is maintained, and of the three republics Georgia is the most prosperous. The Government and the mass of the people are violently anti-communist. But their independence is to them a very real issue, and since Lenin has offered to recognise them as an independent State, it is more than probable that, if the test came, they would recognize the Soviet Government as representing Russia rather than Denikin.

(f.) Relations to the Pan-Turanian Movement.
Pan-Turanian, Turkish, or Pan-Islamic influences play no part in Georgia or Armenia, and by the nature of their

history and their religion, this block of Christian States will always be actively hostile to any Moslem movement. The Georgian Mussulman seems to be primarily Georgian, and his Turkish or Pan-Islamic tendencies are mainly sentimental.

In Azerbaijan and Daghestan, however, matters are different. While neither of these peoples has any desire to come under Turkish domination, in both countries, there is a strong Pan-Islamic movement in existence, and many well-known agitators are at work.

(g.) Relations to Persia.

These are of special importance in the case of Azerbaijan.

The Azerbaijan is of the same religion (Shiah Moslem), and speaks the same Turki language as the Persian inhabitants of the northern provinces of Persia, including Ghilan and Persian Azerbaijan (the name "Azerbaijan" was given to the Republic under Turkish auspices in the expectation that a peace imposed by the Central Powers would provide for the incorporation of Persian Azerbaijan in the Republic).

Business ties between the two countries are, moreover, traditionally close. The effect of this connection, especially since the Anglo-Persian agreement, has been to strengthen the British position in Azerbaijan, which, before launching out into any definite policy, is undoubtedly waiting to judge the real strength and tendencies of British influence in Persia.

Commitments of the Allies towards Transcaucasia.

(a.) Of the Peace Conference.

The Peace Conference have allowed delegates of the republics to come to Paris, and state their case, and have given sympathetic but non-committal replies.

The Supreme Council have also despatched an "Allied High Commissioner for Armenia" (an American officer, Colonel Haskell) to Transcaucasia with his staff.

This mission has concerned itself primarily with relief work, the main burden of which has been borne by the American Relief Commission, an unofficial organisation reported to have expended recently about £600,000 per month in Armenia alone. But it has also exercised a restraining influence on questions of disputed territory and is no doubt; entitled to a share of the credit for the recent arrangements providing for a peaceful settlement of these issues.

(b.) Of the Individual Allies.

The British occupied the principal points in Transcaucasia on the conclusion of the Turkish Armistice. The primary function of our troops was to secure the withdrawal of the Turkish forces from the confines of the former Russian Empire.

When this had been accomplished, and for reasons of economy, the British forces were withdrawn (last August) except from Batoum.

During our occupation, the British Military Command gave local recognition to the various Governments and administrative bodies which they found in existence and announced by proclamation that the occupation was in accordance with the Armistice and that they had no intention of interfering with the internal politics of the country.

No other recognition beyond general messages of sympathy has been granted the republics by His Majesty's Government. But, as already stated, Mr. Wardrop was sent to Tiflis on the withdrawal of our troops with the title of "British Chief Commissioner in Transcaucasia," and with instructions to use his best offices to keep the republics (a) from fighting among themselves, (b) from giving any provocation to General Denikin.

Next to this country among the Allies, the Italians have played the most conspicuous part in Transcaucasia since the Armistice. In the early spring of this year, the Peace Conference offered to entrust the control of these regions to Italy. This was refused after the lapse of some weeks, but an Italian military mission was sent out to Tiflis, where it still is. Meanwhile, there has been a great development of Italian commercial activity, and the Italian Government is considering the idea of supporting the republic's claims to independence in return for the promise of concessions, of which Transcaucasia, rich in oil, timber, coal, and metal ores, can offer enough and spare. The sinister feature in these proceedings is that there is good ground to suppose the Italians to be screening German commercial interests, which are far from reconciled to the permanent loss of the commercial plums secured to them by the German-Georgian Treaty of May-June 1918. German prestige stands high in Georgia owing to the support given against the Turks, and the presence in Georgia for some months before the Armistice of a picked garrison of German troops.

The Transcaucasian Problem.

The Transcaucasian problem is bound up with the greater question of Russia.
This point has been sufficiently brought out in the above notes and need not be laboured.
In the case of Georgia and Azerbaijan, inclusion as autonomous provinces in a federated Russia would be a compromise which need not perhaps be ruled out.
The future of Armenia seems at the present time to depend on whether a mandatory Power can be found to accept the responsibility for watching over her development.
The connection of Transcaucasia with the Turkish settlement is much less close.

The only direct link is the territorial question as regards the new Armenian State, and, less directly, the possible repercussion of the peace terms on Azerbaijan with her Pan-Islamic tendencies.

But, apart from these considerations, Great Britain, as an Eastern Power, cannot disinterest herself from the Transcaucasian settlement. Transcaucasia is one of the most important gateways to the East. Her railways (Batoum-Baku and Batoum-Tiflis-Julfa) lead respectively to the Caspian and so to Krasnovodsk and Turkestan, seething with Bolshevik and Pan-Islamic agitation, and into Persia, where Great Britain has recently assumed new responsibilities. The projected Aliat-Julfa line, originally surveyed by the Russians, and for the construction of which the Azerbaijanis are now seeking foreign assistance, will link up the two systems and allow the currents of trade and propaganda carried by the one to be easily diverted to the other. It would seem essential that the countries through which pass these vital arteries of communication between East and West should be both prosperous and well-disposed to Great Britain and to British policy.

The Question of Recognition.

It must be conceded at once that Armenia is in a different position from Georgia and Azerbaijan in this respect since all the Allied Powers during the war have committed themselves more or less directly to the creation of an independent Armenian State under a European or an American mandate. The only question to be decided in the case of Armenia is the extent of Turkish territory which should be added to the Erivan Republic to make up the new State-

Turning to Georgia and Azerbaijan, the claim of the former to an independent existence is infinitely stronger than that of Azerbaijan. Georgia has had a long history as an independent State and possesses a cohesion and

191

capacity for self-government much superior to those hitherto manifested by the mixed population of Azerbaijan.

The latter, like Daghestan, was for centuries under Persian rule and has no more moral claim to independence than having the inhabitants of the Persian provinces of Ghilan and Azerbaijan. At the same time, it is very difficult, if not impossible, to treat Georgia in one way and Azerbaijan in another. If the Russians are allowed to cross the Caucasus range and occupy Azerbaijan at one end of the Batoum-Baku railway, the liberties of Georgia can never be secure. On the other hand, in the absence of any more definite expression of local opinion in favour of such a course, it would be difficult for His Majesty's Government to consent to the reincorporation of the Republic of Azerbaijan, carrying with it, of course, Baku and its vast oil resources, in Persia. Such a step would be resented more bitterly by Russians of all shades of political opinion than the establishment of Azerbaijan as an independent State.

For practical purposes, it must, therefore, be assumed that the two republics must be treated on the same footing. The problem then becomes largely one of:

(a) How far we are prepared to affront Denikin and the All-Russia party, and

(b) How much importance we attach to the creation of buffer States between Persia and the reconstituted Russia of the future.

An idea which appears to command a considerable amount of sympathy among the advocates of a federated Russia is that the independence of the republics should be immediately recognised by the Allies and that they should be placed under a British or American mandate, pending the formation of the League of Nations. Recognition should be dependent on the agreement of the Republics concerned (including possibly Armenia) to form a federated State and should be followed by a declaration of the mandatory Power's willingness to extend its mandate over any autonomous part of the former Russian Empire, provided its governing body is formed on a democratic basis.

It is anticipated that the immediate effect of this step would be to secure the incorporation of the Don, Terek and Kuban Cossack districts, followed by Ukraine, in the new Federated State. This latter would gradually extend all over the former Russian Empire, forming a democratic federated republic in which there would be no room for Bolshevism.

Action on these lines could hardly fail to bring the mandatory Power into acute conflict with Denikin and the All-Russia Party and to involve responsibilities which no single Allied Power would probably care to undertake at the present time.

Another alternative would be to continue to abstain from recognising the independence of Georgia and Azerbaijan until General Denikin's position becomes more certain, whilst putting pressure on him not to attack either of these two Republics.

A third alternative would be to recognise the independence of Georgia and Azerbaijan forthwith, subject to the decision of the League of Nations in, say, five years' time as to their reincorporation, as autonomous States, in a Russia reconstituted on a federal basis. Prompt action on these lines might possibly restrain General Denikin from employing the winter months in the subjugation of Transcaucasia, which there is every indication that he is at present contemplating.

On the other hand, it may be doubted whether qualified recognition of this kind would be by itself sufficient to force him and the party for which he stands into the arms of Germany.

Foreign Office, December 24, 1919

ANNEX III

Catalogue Reference: CAB/23/35 Image Reference:0004
[…]

THE PRIME MINISTER informed the Conference that he was to meet Clemenceau on the following day, and he wished to consult his colleagues as to the line that he should take.

He himself thought it might be best if he met M. Clemenceau alone, in order that they might clear the air by a frank talk before any Conference was held with other Allied Ministers. It would probably be necessary to invite Signor *(Vittorio)* Scialoja *(Foreign Minister of the Kingdom of Italy)* to some of the meetings, and his own opinion was that it might be as well to send an invitation to the American Ambassador. Unfortunately, the conversations which had hitherto taken place with Signor Scialoja had proved absolutely fruitless, as the Italian Foreign Minister neither had any suggestions to make himself nor had he any authority to accept any suggestions of ours. Mr. Lloyd George said that he attached the greatest importance to a very early meeting, in Italy, England, or elsewhere, of really responsible Ministers with authority to sign Agreements.

THE SECRETARY OF STATE FOR FOREIGN AFFAIRS agreed that an invitation should be sent to Mr. Davis to be present at meetings when Signer Scialoja attended, but he was quite certain that Mr. Davis would be party to no decision. He thought that a number of talks with M. Clemenceau might be more profitable than one prolonged Conference.

It was agreed —

"That invitations should be sent to the American Ambassador and Signor Scialoja to attend certain Conferences to be held in the course of the next few days when the questions of the Adriatic and Turkey were discussed."

THE PRIME MINISTER then asked what he should say to M. Clemenceau.

THE SECRETARY OF STATE FOR FOREIGN AFFAIRS suggested that he should speak rather on the lines of which he had spoken to M. *(Louis)* Loucheur when the latter had lunched with him recently when the Prime Minister had pointed out how things were drifting and how the United States were practically dropped out. He had further complained of the tone of the French Press, which was inspired by the Quai d'Orsay and which was to be deplored at a time when things were so critical.

How was it possible to make Peace in the Middle East when the atmosphere was poisoned by Allied Press attacks? The second point was that things were drawing to a head in Morocco.

The French thought that they had Syria in their hands, that they had squared Feisul, and they now intended to turn Tangier into a French Naval Possession.

A third point to which the Prime Minister might refer was the question of the guarantee of the integrity of French soil.

This was our strongest weapon and should be kept in reserve. Parliament had accepted the guarantee so long as the United States were associated with us, but if we came in alone, it was doubtful whether it would be approved.

He hoped that the two Prime Ministers would not get tangled up with the narrower issues involved, i.e. the borders of Palestine, the Dan-Beersheba line, or the limits of Arab sphere.

As regards Constantinople, was it to remain with the Turk, and, if not, what kind of administration was to be set up? The French had recently changed their attitude; at first, they had wanted to take over the administration of Constantinople.

They had then receded from this position, and then, after the withdrawal of the United States, they had revived the proposal for an Anglo-French administration with an Anglo-French Police Force, and so on, leading to a condominium, which would be a certain source of friction, in his opinion, out of which we should eventually clear with disgust. Lord Curzon said that he was in favour of an International Commission administering Constantinople and the Straits.

If it were necessary to make concessions to Moslem and Indian sentiment, he would transfer the capital of Turkey to Asia Minor and leave the Sultan in a "Vatican" on the Straits. Two further proposals had been made; one was to have definite spheres of economic control for the French, the Italians and the Greeks; and the second, to have one power to control the *[illegible word)* another the customs and so forth.

THE LORD PRESIDENT OF THE COUNCIL said that his own plan was —

(a)   The Greeks to have Smyrna, and

(b)   The Italians to be granted prior economics concessions in the area allotted to them under the Sykes-Picot Agreement.

He did not think it was necessary to work out the details of this at present. That we ourselves really wanted was free ingress for our goods. He reminded the Conference that what we had obtained in Mesopotamia was enormous,

[80] Note that there is no mention here of Sykes-Picot. The Agreement of 1916 was one of various agreements and documents of understanding that the Allies (excluding the USA) had been discussing throughout the war. (*Author's remark*)

whereas the Italians were, in reality, receiving very little. He suggested that we should follow roughly the lines of the Agreement of 1916,[80] which gave Mesopotamia to the British, Syria and Cilicia to the French, and South Asia Minor to the Italians. His own view was that the Italians would accept much less than they were entitled to claim.

THE SECRETARY OF STATE FOR INDIA thought that much depended upon the way in which the negotiations were conducted. He suggested that, in granting concessions to the Italians, care should be taken to avoid any appearance of partitioning up Asia Minor among the Allies. If it was intended to turn Turkey out of Constantinople, he did not think the so-called "Vatican" solution was any real solution so far as Moslem sentiment was concerned. The Moslems did claim the sovereignty, however titular and shadowy, of Constantinople.

He agreed that an International Commission was the right solution, but he would have a Treaty with the Turks forcing the Sultan to have Constantinople and the Straits administered by a Commission in the Sultan's name.

He was anxious to know what it was proposed to do with Adrianople. The further one went North of the Straits the more Turkish the population became. Briefly, he agreed entirely with Mr. Balfour about Italy, and he did not quarrel with the suggestion that the Greeks should be given Smyrna, and he agreed with the Foreign Secretary about an international control of the Straits so long as the titular sovereignty of Constantinople remained with the Turks.

THE SECRETARY OF STATE FOR WAR said that he earnestly trusted that the conversations with M. Clemenceau would be profitable. Any solution was better than no solution. He thought that the Prime Minister should say that, as the United States have now gone out, the matter is simplified; and if only France and England can reach agreement on Turkish policy, with a fair recognition of Italian claims, we could make that agreement effective.

France would be consternated if she learned that it was by no means a foregone conclusion that we would guarantee her integrity, and he agreed with Lord Curzon that this was a very powerful weapon in our hands.

Today the Turkish control was passing from our hands. We controlled Constantinople on both sides of the Straits, but not the huge territories lying outside it. There was a real danger of Bolshevist penetration, imperiling our interests in the Middle East. Another reason why it was important to come to an early agreement with the French was that our troops in Turkey were deteriorating in quality and they had to be relieved by young, immature men.

The French had great interests in Constantinople, and so we ought to be able to square them. It was vital to come to some definite agreement between the two Great Powers concerned. He was in favour of what would virtually be an Anglo-French Administration, with certain concessions to other Powers. Next, he had reason to believe that M. Clemenceau intended to discuss Russia. The situation there deteriorated every day. If nothing could be done, we ought to clear out. He reminded the Conference that a month previously the Prime Minister had practically given an assurance to the House of Commons that the Russian question would be finally settled at this Conference. As with Turkey, so with Russia; there must be a joint definite Anglo-French policy.

We must decide —

(a) That orders were to be given to The Baltic States:

(b) That we were to do in regard to Poland:

(c) Are we to adopt the Sahinkoff policy of a Conference between the anti-Bolshevik States and the loyal Russians, with Great Britain and France supervising?

If there were much further delay, Lenin and Trotsky would prevail. England and France must speak with one voice, in respect of Finland, the Baltic States, the loyal Russians, and so on.

198

THE PRESIDENT OF THE BOARD OF EDUCATION
said that he was much attracted by Mr. Balfour's suggestion
for South Asia Minor, but as regards North Asia Minor and
Armenia we had a strong body of opinion in England which
was anti-Turk, which we might attract by showing that we
had taken proper precautions to ensure the protection of
Armenia.

As regards Constantinople and the Straits, he favoured an
International Commission to control the Straits and to
exercise effective control over Constantinople, with the
Sultan in nominal control. Indian students with whom he
had come in contact were very apprehensive of the effect in
India of the expulsion of Turkey from Constantinople.

THE SECRETARY OF STATE FOR FOREIGN
AFFAIRS thought that if the French remained in Asia
Minor, we might argue that it was up to them to look after
the whole of the Armenians on the coast and in the strip
connecting with Russian Armenia, near Erivan. An
alternative had been suggested by Lord Bryce, who had
said that if we could persuade some great or small Power to
take charge of Armenia, the United States would supply the
necessary funds, although they might shrink from political
responsibility.

As regards Mr. Fisher's other point, he did not believe that
there was any serious or lasting sentiment in England about
expulsion.

THE LORD PRESIDENT OF THE COUNCIL said that
Mr. Churchill's view was that the Prime Minister should
come to some agreement with M. Clemenceau, and then,
say to the rest of the world that we could not tolerate
anarchy in the Middle East, that France and Great Britain
were in agreement, and that the other Powers must
conform.

This would involve the exclusion of the Italians, who might
be a great nuisance, but it was not wise to ignore them.
Owing to their great increase of population as compared

with France, they imagined themselves to be a Great Power. Moreover, they felt ill-used over the Treaty of London, and there was no doubt that the French had behaved badly towards then. We could not, in his opinion, settle Asia Minor without reference to Italy, and it would be impolitic to thrust her ostentatiously into the background. He agreed that there could be no Inter-Allied Conference in London during the next two or three days.

What was required was a Conference of much bigger scope than was possible here, with more extended time. We might tell the French that they had made Paris impossible, that we do not insist upon London, and that we suggest that the Conference should meet in Brussels.

As regards Constantinople he was inclined to agree with Lord Curzon. The place was no part of Moslem religion, but only of Moslem sentiment.

In any Agreement, he hoped it might be possible to exhibit Italy, at any rate nominally, on equal terms with France; her intrigues would no doubt continue, but they would not be effective. Some Agreement which could be reached with M. Clemenceau was devoutly to be desired.

THE LORD PRIVY SEAL said he agreed with Mr. Balfour as regards the Italians. We ought first to come to some clear agreement with M. Clemenceau and then bring in the Italians. In regard to Constantinople, both the Aga Khan and Lord Sinha in Paris had attached great importance to Moslem sentiment.

There was no object, he thought, in taking it from the Turks and handing it over entirely to international control. We could get all we wanted by an International Commission working through a titular Sovereign in Constantinople.

THE PRIME MINISTER thought that about 30,000 international troops would be required to occupy the Straits. It was undesirable that the Sultan should have anything more than a handful of guards himself. Were we to make the Sultan like the Khedive, or was he to be independent, like the Shah of Persia? The latter alternative he thought was dangerous.

Although, as Mr. Montagu had said, the population northwards towards Adrianople was mainly Turkish, the people outside Constantinople proper were overwhelmingly Greek. He thought that we should treat the Sultan as another Khedive and keep him in Constantinople.

THE SECRETARY OF STATE FOR FOREIGN AFFAIRS thought that if the Sultan was left in Constantinople, the Moslem world would say that we had never really defeated him, and he would become at once the center of reaction and future trouble. We thought we should try and settle the future of Constantinople, not from the point of view of India, but of the future of the world.

THE LORD PRIVY SEAL did not agree but thought that we should look at the question mainly from the point of view of the future of, and how it affected, the British Empire.

If we could satisfy the Turks that we intended to treat them well, it would benefit us in India, Mesopotamia, and Egypt.

THE PRIME MINISTER thought that they should consider the practical result of the policies suggested. If the Sultan was at Constantinople, his Ministers must be there.

He would then govern Turkey from Constantinople, where we could only allow him a small bodyguard.

This would mean that he would be the creature of what was really a foreign junta. There was the danger that the French would always try to influence him, and we should have a revival of the old Greek Empire in a much worse form. Constantinople would become a source of infection and war. In his view, the Turk ought to have a chance of making a Turkish Kingdom or community.

This he could not do if he remained under an International Commission, the effect of which would be to turn Turkey into an Egypt worse than the Egypt of the old days, as the

Italians, as well as the French, would be concerned with its administration. He admitted the peril of Moslem and Indian sentiment, but he would say to the Turk: - "Go to Bursa, where you can be independent. As Turkey must govern the Straits, they must be guarded by an international force. The closing of the Straits by Turkey during the war had prolonged the war by two years, and Turkey had thus signally failed in her duty to the world." The Turk was in the minority in Constantinople itself, and much more so in the suburbs.

THE SECRETARY OF STATE FOR INDIA asked whether the Prime Minister would consider a plebiscite of the population of Thrace, on the lines of the Polish plebiscite.

THE PRIME MINISTER pointed out that the cases were rather different. Danzig was 95 percent German, but as it was the door of Poland, we could not leave it to Germany.

Constantinople was the door between Europe and Asia and must be internationalized. Further, with her great populations, Turkey was a different problem from Egypt, where the population was practically entirely on the banks of the Nile.

THE SECRETARY OF STATE FOR INDIA said he wished it placed on record that all Indian opinion in London and India, official and native, was against the proposed solution. It would be quite impossible to use Indian troops to enforce a Peace of this kind.

THE LORD PRIVY SEAL again emphasized the importance of conciliating Turkish opinion.

THE SECRETARY OF STATE FOR WAR said the Conference had formed certain quite clear proposals:
(a) That Constantinople should be internationalized:

(b) That the Sultan should reside there as a titular head:
(c) That the government of Turkey should be exercised from Brusa,[81] where the Sultan's Ministers would be, with Allied Commissioners to advise them.

THE PRIME MINISTER said that in this way the Yildiz Kiosk would be the Sultan's Vatican. He reminded the Conference that today there was a Commission governing Constantinople in the Sultan's name.

THE PRESIDENT OF THE BOARD OF EDUCATION said he agreed with Mr. Churchill's suggestion as tending to conciliate Turkish and Moslem sentiment. It would be a great advantage to us if we could make the Turks feel that we had played up for them.

THE LORD PRIVY SEAL asked which solution was likely to give less trouble to us in Egypt, India, and Mesopotamia?

THE SECRETARY OF STATE FOR INDIA said he would withdraw his objection if the government was to be from Brusa in the name of the Sultan, who would have the power to reside in Constantinople. He again enquired what was to be done about Adrianople.

THE SECRETARY OF STATE FOR FOREIGN AFFAIRS replied that early in the year it had been proposed in Paris that there should be an international State there. In regard to Mr. Montagu's statement about the unanimity of Indian opinion, he said that all the Indian officials in the Middle East were strongly in favour of the dissolution of the Turkish Empire and of turning the Turks out of Constantinople.

---

[81] Brusa is located on the northwestern Anatolia, within the region of Marmara.

THE SECRETARY OF STATE FOR WAR foresaw danger in letting the Sultan be in Brusa, where he would gradually collect round him Mustapha Kemal, Enver, Trotsky, and others, who would help him build up a huge hostile force and turn Asia Minor and Arabia into a seething cauldron of trouble.

(a) That Constantinople should be internationalized:

(b) That the Sultan should reside there as a titular head:

(c) That the government of Turkey should be exercised from Brusa, where the Sultan's Ministers would be, with Allied Commissioners to advise them.

THE PRIME MINISTER said that in this way the Yildiz Kiosk would be the Sultan's Vatican. He reminded the Conference that today there was a Commission governing Constantinople in the Sultan's name.

THE PRESIDENT OF THE BOARD OF EDUCATION said he agreed with Mr. Churchill's suggestion, as tending to conciliate Turkish and Moslem sentiment. It would be a great advantage to us if we could make the Turks feel that we had played up for them.

THE LORD PRIVY SEAL asked which solution was likely to give less trouble to us in Egypt, India, and Mesopotamia?

THE SECRETARY OF STATE FOR INDIA said he would withdraw his objection if the government was to be from Brusa in the name of the Sultan, who would have the power to reside in Constantinople. He again enquired what was to be done about Adrianople.

THE SECRETARY OF STATE FOR FOREIGN AFFAIRS replied that early in the year it had been proposed in Paris that there should be an international State there. In regard to Mr. Montagu's statement about the unanimity of Indian opinion, he said that all the Indian officials in the Middle East were strongly in favour of the dissolution of the Turkish Empire and of turning the Turks out of Constantinople.

THE SECRETARY OF STATE FOR WAR foresaw danger in letting the Sultan be in Brusa, where he would gradually collect round him Mustapha Kemal, Enver, Trotsky, and others, who would help him build up a huge hostile force, and turn Asia Minor and Arabia into a seething cauldron of trouble.

It would be wise, in his opinion, to keep him in Constantinople, under our eye. However, he was quite prepared to support anything that was agreed upon by the Prime Minister and M. Clemenceau.

THE LORD PRIVY SEAL thought that the Prime Minister might put it to M. Clemenceau: "What is most likely to bring peace to the British Empire and peace in Europe?"

THE PRIME MINISTER said the point was that the Alliance that won the War was now falling to pieces.

The United States were dropping away, Italy was recalcitrant, and France and ourselves were agreed on no subject. France wanted to adopt Bismarck's attitude, which nearly brought on the war in 1874.

It was essential for us to have a complete understanding with France on all these vital problems. It was disastrous that the Peace Conference had been held in Paris, where a Press campaign against us had been sedulously worked by the Quai d'Orsay, and even M. Clemenceau had been overborne. Moreover, Signor Orlando's constant absence, with his Foreign Minister, meant that popular opinion in Italy had gone to pieces. He would like to revert to the practice adopted by the Supreme War Council, which was, that the Allied Ministers met in their several countries in turn.

THE SECRETARY OF STATE FOR FOREIGN AFFAIRS thought that M. Clemenceau's point was that he must keep up the prestige of France by having the Conferences in Paris, especially because the British were everywhere *en evidence* in the Middle East; but he agreed with the Prime Minister that Paris as the meeting place had really smashed the Alliance. He himself would like to have the Conference somewhere where could be assembled all the Ministers who could decide fundamentals. The fundamentals to be decided were:

(i) Our general policy in Russia:
(ii) Asia Minor and the question of Mandates:
(iii) Is the Turk to be in or outside Constantinople?

As regards the Conference to settle these questions, he would
like to see it meet in London.

THE SECRETARY OF STATE FOR WAR agreed with this latter suggestion, on the understanding that the final ratification should take place in Paris.

THE PRIME MINISTER wondered whether it would be possible to get really responsible Italian Ministers to come to London. The first point he would make with M. Clemenceau, he thought, was the necessity of bringing the Alliance together again.

THE PRESIDENT OF THE BOARD OF EDUCATION thought that the Conference were generally agreed, except for a difference of opinion as to the extent of the nominal power to be vested in the Sultan.

The Conference ended at 7:15 p.m. *(It began at 5:00 p.m.)*
Whitehall Gardens, S.W. 1, December 10, 1919.

ANNEX IV

President Woodrow Wilson's Fourteen Points

8 January 1918:
President Woodrow Wilson's Fourteen Points

It will be our wish and purpose that the processes of peace, when they are begun, shall be absolutely open and that they shall involve and permit no secret understandings of any kind henceforth. The day of conquest and aggrandizement is gone by; so is also the day of secret covenants entered into in the interest of particular governments and likely at some unlooked-for moment to upset the peace of the world. It is this happy fact, now clear to the view of every public man whose thoughts do not still linger in an age that is dead and gone, which makes it possible for every nation whose purposes are consistent with justice and the peace of the world to avow nor or at any other time the objects it has in view.

We entered this war because violations of right had occurred which touched us to the quick and made the life of our own people impossible unless they were corrected and the world secure once for all against their recurrence. What we demand in this war, therefore, is nothing peculiar to ourselves. It is that the world be made fit and safe to live in; and particularly that it be made safe for every peace-loving nation which, like our own, wishes to live its own life, determine its own institutions, be assured of justice and fair dealing by the other peoples of the world as against force and selfish aggression. All the peoples of the world are in effect partners in this interest, and for our own part we see very clearly that unless justice be done to others it will not be done to us. The programme of the world's peace, therefore, is our programme; and that programme, the only possible programme, as we see it, is this:

I. Open covenants of peace, openly arrived at, after which there shall be no private international understandings of any kind, but diplomacy shall always proceed frankly and in the public view.

II. Absolute freedom of navigation upon the seas, outside territorial waters, alike in peace and in war, except as the seas may be closed in whole or in part by international action for the enforcement of international covenants.

III. The removal, so far as possible, of all economic barriers and the establishment of an equality of trade conditions among all the nations consenting to the peace and associating themselves for its maintenance.

IV. Adequate guarantees given and taken that national armaments will be reduced to the lowest point consistent with domestic safety.

V. A free, open-minded, and absolutely impartial adjustment of all colonial claims, based upon a strict observance of the principle that in determining all such questions of sovereignty the interests of the populations concerned must have equal weight with the equitable claims of the government whose title is to be determined.

VI. The evacuation of all Russian territory and such a settlement of all questions affecting Russia as will secure the best and freest cooperation of the other nations of the world in obtaining for her an unhampered and unembarrassed opportunity for the independent determination of her own political development and national policy and assure her of a sincere welcome into the society of free nations under institutions of her own choosing; and, more than a welcome, assistance also of every kind that she may need and may herself desire.

The treatment accorded Russia by her sister nations in the months to come will be the acid test of their good will, of their comprehension of her needs as distinguished from their own interests, and of their intelligent and unselfish sympathy.

VII. Belgium, the whole world will agree, must be evacuated and restored, without any attempt to limit the sovereignty which she enjoys in common with all other free nations.

No other single act will serve as this will serve to restore confidence among the nations in the laws which they have themselves set and determined for the government of their relations with one another. Without this healing act the whole structure and validity of international law is forever impaired.

VIII. All French territory should be freed and the invaded portions restored, and the wrong done to France by Prussia in 1871 in the matter of Alsace-Lorraine, which has unsettled the peace of the world for nearly fifty years, should be righted, in order that peace may once more be made secure in the interest of all.

IX. A readjustment of the frontiers of Italy should be effected along clearly recognizable lines of nationality.

X. The peoples of Austria-Hungary, whose place among the nations we wish to see safeguarded and assured, should be accorded the freest opportunity to autonomous development.

XI. Rumania, Serbia, and Montenegro should be evacuated; occupied territories restored; Serbia accorded free and secure access to the sea; and the relations of the several Balkan states to one another determined by friendly counsel along historically established lines of allegiance and nationality; and international guarantees of the political and economic independence and territorial integrity of the several Balkan states should be entered into.

XII. The Turkish portion of the present Ottoman Empire should be assured a secure sovereignty, but the other nationalities which are now under Turkish rule should be assured an undoubted security of life and an absolutely unmolested opportunity of autonomous development, and the Dardanelles should be permanently opened as a free passage to the ships and commerce of all nations under international guarantees.

XIII. An independent Polish state should be erected which should include the territories inhabited by indisputably Polish populations, which should be assured a free and secure access to the sea, and whose political and economic independence and territorial integrity should be guaranteed by international covenant.

XIV. A general association of nations must be formed under specific covenants for the purpose of affording mutual guarantees of political independence and territorial integrity to great and small states alike.

In regard to these essential rectifications of wrong and assertions of right we feel ourselves to be intimate partners of all the governments and peoples associated together against the Imperialists.

We cannot be separated in interest or divided in purpose. We stand together until the end.

For such arrangements and covenants we are willing to fight and to continue to fight until they are achieved; but only because we wish the right to prevail and desire a just and stable peace such as can be secured only by removing the chief provocations to war, which this programme does remove.

We have no jealousy of German greatness, and there is nothing in this programme that impairs it.

We grudge her no achievement or distinction of learning or of pacific enterprise such as have made her record very bright and very enviable.

We do not wish to injure her or to block in any way her legitimate influence or power. We do not wish to fight her either with arms or with hostile arrangements of trade if she is willing to associate herself with us and the other peace-loving nations of the world in covenants of justice and law and fair dealing.

We wish her only to accept a place of equality among the peoples of the world, -- the new world in which we now live, -- instead of a place of mastery.

INDEX

Orlando, Vittorio, 57, 133, 142

Paleologue, Maurice 38
Palestine, 15-20, 22-25, 29-31, 34, 41, 50, 53, 54, 55, 60, 61, 64-67, 71, 74, 76, 77, 82, 88, 92, 100, [Samuel Herbert and Rufus Isaacs {Lord Reading, 103}104-111, 117, 119, 121, 125, 195
Pan-Arabism, 41, 131, 132
Pichon, Stephen, 57
Picot, Georges, 6, 7, 11, 28,30, 32, 37,42, 43, 44, 45, 48, 51, 59, 64, 65,67, 68, 69, 70, 71, 72, 88, 98, 104, 112, 118, 134, 144, 145, 147, 148, 151, 152. 153, 157
Poincaré, Henri, 139, 141

Racism, 19 [*races*, 18, 20, 127, 128, 150, 172, 175]
Railroad, 15, 16, 52, 59, 100, 101 [Railway, 15, 16,52, 59, 100, 101]

Sarrail, Maurice 91, 92
Sazonov, Sergey (Sasonoff), 38
Sonnino, Sidney, 57
Sultan Abdul Hamid II, 16
Sykes, Mark, 6-17, 20, 23-31, 36, 43, 45, 46, 48, 50, 59, 61, 71-79, 83-88, 95, 98, 100, 104, 107, 116, 117, 118, 119, 124-129, 131, 134, 143-148, 152, 153, 196, 215
Sykes, Mark, 6, 8, 9, 10, 11, 12, 14, 15, 16, 17, 18, 19, 20, 21, 22, 23, 25, 27, 28, 30, 32, 37, 42, 44, 45, 49, 50, 51, 65, 67, 72, 98, 112, 119, 134, 143, 145, 147, 148, 151, 157
Sykes-Picot, 6, 24, 25, 26, 28, 29, 30, 31, 36, 45, 46, 59, 61, 71, 72, 74, 75, 76, 79, 83-88, 95, 100, 107, 116, 117, 118, 119, 124, 125, 128, 129, 131, 134, 143-148, 152, 196, 215

Versailles, 51, 74, 75, 88, 89, 97, 99, 100, 129, 130, 131, 143-148

Weizmann, Chaim, 105, 106
Wilson, Woodrow, 44, 56, 57, 58, 59, 61, 80, 81, 96, 97, 98, 99, 100, 101, 102, 103, 107, 124, 133, 142, 144, 145, 146, 147, 207

By the same Author

Middle East Perspective – Personal Recollection 1947-1967.

Middle East Perspectives; - From Lebanon 1968-1988.

Much Pain Little Gain – Lebanon 1968-1976.

Lebanon in Flames. Still Battling High 1977-1988.

Shouting in the Wilderness - Lebanon 1989-1998.

On A Razor Edge - Lebanon 1998-2006.

A King Oppressed – The Story of Farouk I of Egypt, 1936-1952.

Turkey's Last Century of Trouble – 1824-1924.

Sykes-Picot – 1916. Acting for the dotted line.

Egypt: A Tough Nut to Crack: Nasser 1952-1956.

Nasser's Sense of Status: 1957-1961.

The Last Chapter: Nasser 1962-1970.

CPSIA information can be obtained
at www.ICGtesting.com
Printed in the USA
LVHW082255270922
729455LV00033B/916

9 781548 039769